Copyright © 2021 by Genevieve Mckay

All rights reserved.

No part of this book may be reproduced in any form or by any electronic or mechanical means, including information storage and retrieval systems, without written permission from the author, except for the use of brief quotations in a book review.

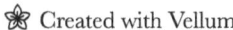 Created with Vellum

A GREYSTONE
MANOR
MYSTERY

The *Curse* of the *Golden Touch*

GENEVIEVE McKAY

THE CURSE OF THE GOLDEN TOUCH

GENEVIEVE MCKAY

StonePony Studios

Chapter 1

"You treat that horse like an oversized dog, Jillian," Mother said from the open window of her charcoal-grey Lexus. She arched her thinly plucked eyebrows disapprovingly at Bally, who was grazing placidly nearby, then shifted her sharp gaze toward me.

I looked away, avoiding the argument she was obviously dying to start, and scuffed the toe of my leather boot against the frozen ground, upturning a few clods of dirt. Cold morning air stung my cheeks and my breath plumed out in a cloud. I pushed any trace of anger down firmly. There was no winning a debate with my mother, the best tactic was either to ignore or distract her.

Beyond the car, the sun made its first push up over the horizon, spreading a tinge of pink across the rolling hills and lighting up the delicate layer of frost that outlined every blade of grass and russet leaf like the late autumn landscape had been dipped in sugar. Fall was my favourite time of year; everything seemed to have a touch of magic cast over it somehow.

Mother huffed out a column of frosty air, irritated by my silence, and pulled her heavy mink coat tighter around her thin frame. A strand of jet-black hair nearly escaped from under her matching fur turban before she ruthlessly tucked it away. Nothing annoyed her more than disorder. She had the look of an aging film star from the 1920s. Even at this hour, her face was perfectly made up, right down to the blood-red lipstick and dark smoky eyes, as if she were poised to take center stage.

"Imported dressage horses from Germany should not be walking around the estate, loose, like tame circus ponies," she said finally, trying to needle me again. "He has important competitions coming up. You should be focused on your training. Or at the very least, you should not be traipsing around the property at all hours like a lost soul. You need to think of your future, Jillian."

"Yes, Mother," I said, automatically side-stepping her disapproval like I had every day for the last twenty years of my life. "But Bally is nearly as clever as a circus pony, aren't you, boy?"

I looked over at the big horse fondly, smiling as he carefully plucked the last frozen red berries off a rosehip bush. Besides being a talented dressage horse, Bally had a variety of tricks that I'd taught him over the years. He could shake hands … er, hooves … and nod his head yes and no when you pretended to ask him a question, he could bow on command, and he'd even taught himself to open his stall door and sneak outside when nobody was looking. "Besides, he loves our morning walks; Christoph says they're good for him."

"*Chris*toph." Mother wrinkled the tip of her elegant nose as if she'd smelled something bad. Our head trainer, Christoph, and Mother had a love-hate relationship that had spanned the last fifteen years. They disagreed on nearly everything and she only kept him on because our horses looked fantastic under his care and won pretty much every competition they entered.

"Never mind all that," she said dismissively, waving a gloved hand in my direction. "I didn't come all the way out here at this ungodly hour to argue. Your cousin is here. He wants to see you."

"Which cousin?" I asked warily. My many choices in cousins ranged from friendly and fun to borderline insane.

Mother sighed heavily and put one hand wearily over her eyes as if our brief conversation had taxed the last of her strength.

"I can't be expected to waste all my time answering your endless questions, Jillian. Move along. I left him eating eggs in the kitchen. I honestly don't know why you can't be more like your cousin Viola over at Lime Tree. You don't see her trooping around in the wilderness like a hobo before sunrise. After she schools the ponies, she stays in the house and has cocktails like a civilized human being."

She sent another despairing look at Bally, rolled up her window, and peeled away like a race car driver in the direction of the house, tires spinning on the loose gravel.

"Because Cousin Viola is the most boring, vapid human being on the planet," I whispered rebelliously after the retreating car. "And she drinks like a fish."

Which wasn't quite fair; Viola was okay in her own way; we just didn't have much in common. Besides the Welsh ponies she bred and trained, she liked to talk about three things: money, men, and men who had money. It got a little tedious after a while. But, even after all these years, it still stung me the tiniest bit that she was exactly the sort of daughter Mother wished I'd been.

"Come on, handsome, I guess we'll have to cut our walk short this morning."

Bally popped his head up out the shrub he'd been rooting around in and harrumphed, giving me an offended look.

"I'm sorry, I'll make it up to you later." I ran my hand down his silky grey neck and adjusted the front of the thick, red-plaid stable blanket he always wore on frosty mornings. It had shifted to one side during our trek up the hill, giving him a rakish air.

Impulsively, I reached out and kissed him on his silvery nose, admiring for the millionth time how truly beautiful he was. Bally was one of those rare dapple-grey horses whose colour hadn't yet faded as he aged. His dapples were vivid starbursts of white over a background of smoky gun-metal grey. He had dark, intelligent eyes, and the proudly arched neck and broad, well-muscled back that were the hallmark of good breeding combined with many years of careful schooling.

Bally had been there with me through thick and thin, starting when I was a shy teenager right through my short-lived engagement to awful Fredrick. When my marriage plans had come to such a disastrous (and so very, very public) end, Bally had been my calm in the storm.

He and I had been sneaking in these pre-breakfast walks since I'd brought him home from Europe as a clumsy, uncoordinated two-year-old. He'd been a present from my father one year and we'd spent nearly every minute of our lives together from the moment he set foot on the property. I'd even trained him to follow me loose like a dog without needing a halter or lead rope. It was effective most of the time ... unless he happened to discover something more interesting than me.

As if guessing my thoughts, he lifted his head high in the air and pricked his ears, staring intently in the direction of our barn. A hopeful whinny escaped him and he worked his jaw in a slight chewing motion as if he were imagining eating something tasty. Far away, I could just make out the sounds of the other horses getting fed their breakfast grain; buckets rattled, stall doors slid open, and horses nickered eagerly in anticipation.

"Wait, Bally," I said, fumbling with the empty halter in my hand, but it was too late. His eyes lit up, he made an excited chortling sound under his breath and, before I could stop him, he took off past me in a trundling trot in the direction of the stables. His long, silver tail streamed behind him like a banner.

"Well, fine then," I called to his plump, retreating hindquarters. "Suit yourself. I'll go get my own breakfast then. Don't blame me if Christoph gives you a long lecture in Czech when you get back."

The estate was fully fenced; there was nowhere for a horse to escape, and food-loving Bally would inevitably head directly inside the barn for his breakfast, so I wasn't too worried. I knew Christoph, or his son Gilbert, would tuck Bally safely in his stall.

Sighing at the unwelcome interruption to my morning routine, I trudged downhill before turning up the lane toward the modest ten-bedroom bungalow that was Greystone Manor, my childhood home.

Make that ten bedrooms, fifteen bathrooms, two libraries, plus countless living and sitting rooms. Not to mention the billiard room, the conservatory, the sunken indoor pool, and my father's sprawling office that had its own miniature putting green. All set in a rambling grey, stone fortress that looked like it should have a moat and a dungeon (it didn't).

I avoided the huge wooden front doors with their snarling gargoyle brass knockers and instead went around to the side kitchen entrance, inhaling deeply as the smell of coffee, freshly baked biscuits and bacon hit me before I'd even opened the door. The homey yellow-bricked kitchen was my favourite room in the entire house. Growing up, Gilbert and I had spent many blissful hours there with my old Scottish Nanny and our cook Betty, listening to their stories while we ate cookies or did our homework by the fireplace.

Dropping the empty halter beside the stone steps, I pushed at the well-worn door and cautiously peered inside, half-dreading which cousin I might find.

My ancestors had outdone themselves in the baby-making

department. My great-grandmother on my mother's side had had fourteen sisters and most of them had had seven or eight children of their own. And of course, most of *those* children had had children and so on, which left me with more cousins and assorted relatives than I could shake a stick at. I'd long given up keeping track of them all, especially when Mother was often involved in bitter, long-running feuds with one family member or another.

But this time I was in luck.

"If you don't get your filthy boots off this table instantly, *Mister* Xan, I'll remove them myself. Permanently."

I paused just inside the doorway, wincing at Betty's withering tone. She was a no-nonsense sort of cook who'd been with the family longer than I'd been alive and had no problem telling anyone off. Even Mother was afraid of her, though of course, she pretended not to be.

"Now, Betty, don't get your knickers in a twist," Xan teased, leaning far back on the hind legs of his chair and wiggling the heels of his immaculate riding boots on the ancient wooden table. His dark hair was slicked back, and he was clean-shaven and smelled strongly of cologne—a sure sign that he was about to hit someone up for money or a favour. He nudged his plate of eggs dangerously close to the edge of the table, stabbing at the runny yolk with his fork. Then he caught sight of me.

"Canadian cousin!" Xan called, using his silly nickname for me. He was from the American branch of our family and always pretended to make fun of my non-existent accent. His own accent on the other hand was a mix of upper state New York, boarding-school Swiss and the strange, ancient timbre that almost all our relatives shared. It made us sound foreign and exotic; and also, snootier than we had to be. It had made me a target for unlimited teasing and bullying when I was a kid and I'd done my best to stamp every last trace of it out of my own voice.

Xan dropped his feet to the floor and sprang up to meet me, his brown eyes alight with genuine happiness. "You look ravishing as usual."

"Xander," I said happily, throwing my arms around his neck and giving him a solid kiss on the cheek. "You look great too. Where's Mother?"

"Probably back in her crypt, the old hag," Xan muttered and then yelped when Betty smacked him upside the head with a wooden spoon.

"Xander," Betty said warningly, "you'd better have finished your breakfast and vacated my kitchen by the time I get back. I mean it." She sent him a stern look and then stomped out, still brandishing the spoon.

"Try to be nice, Xan."

"I can't," he said happily, sitting back down at the table and pulling me into the wooden chair beside his. "It's not in my nature. Which is why I need your help."

"I thought you were up to something," I said, helping myself to a toasted biscuit off his plate. "Are you here so I can give you, yet another, lesson in manners?"

"No ... well, yes, sort of. Do you remember Great Aunt Ruth?"

"Ugh, how could I forget?" I had a sudden vision of a scowling, grey-haired lady telling me to "man-up" because I was a weak rider who "rode like a girl." An insult that had baffled me because most of the top riders I knew were women. "She tripped me with her cane when I was ten and I had to spend Christmas in a cast. I remember it like it was yesterday."

"Yes, that's her. We used to call her Great Aunt Ruthless, remember? Rich. Reclusive. Bitter. Rich as sin. Childless. Did I mention rich?"

"Several times."

"That's where I need your help, Jilly."

I frowned and sat up abruptly, putting plenty of space between us. "Xan," I said sternly, "I'm not sure where you're going with this, but I'm not going to help you take money from anyone. I'm sorry if your parents' death left you poor…"

"Now, now, Jilly, don't get yourself all worked up. I'm not exactly destitute you know, we orphans still have that drafty old mansion to roam around in and enough money to keep us in horses. And I'm not trying to steal fortunes from helpless old ladies if that's what you're worried about. She's invited me to visit her estate in Quebec, is all, and I don't want to go alone."

"Ooh," I said, relieved and curious. Great Aunt Ruth was ultra-reclusive to the point of being a hermit; she came to stay with us at Christmas occasionally, but other than that she kept in strict hiding. In her youth, she'd evented for the Canadian Equestrian Team. She had been in line to be the first woman to event for Canada at the Olympics, but there'd been some sort of scandal and she'd dropped right off the map. After years of travel, she'd finally settled down on her parents' massive estate in northern Quebec to quietly breed sport horses. Her place was far off the beaten path and hardly anyone in our family had stepped foot on her property. Certainly, *I'd* never been invited to stay. "Really? That's fantastic, Xan. She must actually like you."

"I can't imagine why, unless it's because I'm strikingly handsome, witty and look extra nice in tight breeches."

"That must be it," I said, not bothering to stifle my laughter, "but Xan, why are you here instead of there, then?"

"Nerves," he said dramatically, "she's an extremely intimidating old lady and I don't want to go alone. Just look at this letter."

He pulled a thick wad of paper out of his pocket and slapped it down on the table between us.

I unfolded the stiff paper carefully. *Dear Boy*, it said in large, slashing letters. *It is of utmost importance that you come to Dark Lady Farm immediately. There are things you must know. Disobey me at your peril. Bring your best horses.*

Beneath the words, there was a hastily drawn sketch of a cloaked woman on a rearing horse. I ran my fingers lightly over the ink drawing where the pen had dug in so deeply that it had nearly torn the thick paper. It was a curious thing to add to a letter, I hadn't thought of Great Aunt Ruth as having any artistic leanings.

"Bring your best horses?" I said in confusion, reading the letter again. "Disobey me at your peril? What kind of letter is this?"

"A scary one," Xan said solemnly, "She's hinted a few times in the past that I might be in line to inherit something from her. She's always liked that I event. I never put much weight in her promises since she's crazy as a loon but maybe she wants to sponsor my bid for the Olympics or something."

I nodded encouragingly but secretly thought that Xan had less than a zero chance of ever making it to the Olympics. He was a decent rider of course, but he liked sleeping in and lounging around by the pool far too much to ever train seriously, and he couldn't be bothered to look for sponsors. It took a pretty high focus and drive to make it in any sort of international competition, let alone the Olympics.

"Xan, this letter is dated the fifteenth of August. That was weeks ago."

"Well, I doubt she expected me to drop everything and rush to her side. I had to find a suitable horse, after all."

"It sounds to me like she wanted you to come right away."

"I think that's just how cranky, old people always sound. Now you see why I don't want to go alone, though. Don't you remember the Christmas she had Alastair in tears?"

I did remember. Vividly. Despite the fact that they disliked each other with the intensity of frothing rabid foxes, my mother's family insisted on getting together at least once a year for a holiday filled with stony disapproval, heavy drinking, and sometimes outright brawls.

On the years when Great Aunt Ruth spent Christmas at Greystone Manor, she always delighted in planting herself in a heavy armchair right by the Christmas tree, within striking distance of all the young cousins with her cane. She'd drink endless glasses of gin and make snide comments at anyone who dared slink close enough to collect their presents. She'd never liked me much and she'd grudgingly tolerated Xan, but her hatred of Xan's older siblings, my sly, creepy cousins Sally and Alastair, knew no bounds.

She'd nearly started a brawl one year when she'd accused Alastair of cheating at cards. She'd loudly proclaimed in front of everyone that he was a fraud who would end up penniless like their fortune-losing father, which was quite possibly the worst insult anyone could hurl in our family.

"That was awful," I said sympathetically, remembering how upset Xan and Sally had been, not to mention the colossal tantrum Alastair had thrown. Even though he'd been a grown man by that point, Alastair had burst into tears of rage, kicked over the tree and stuffed half the presents into the fireplace, including mine which thankfully had been a new bathrobe rather than the puppy I'd been hoping for.

"Well, it was the truth, too. My parents did muck everything up. I don't know how they lost their Touch, but it ruined everything."

"Oh, Xan, not that silly old superstition again," I said, rolling my eyes.

The thing with our family is that we're all incredibly lucky. It's sort of a mandatory part of being part of the clan, I suppose. Going back as far as anyone can remember, we had a reputation when it came to investments, business dealings and well, pretty much anything one of us put our hand to. Among the more superstitious members of the family, it's referred to as the Golden Touch.

In Mother and Father's case, it meant that they owned nearly the entire town of nearby Maplegrove and the surrounding farms and forests. Which, I can tell you, did nothing to endear our family to the local townsfolk.

There had always been silly rumours that our luck was due to some weird magical influence but I didn't believe that. There is always a rational, scientific explanation for anything if you look hard enough. My theory is that if you're born incredibly rich and you're raised from infancy to believe that you have a gift, or a Golden Touch, that makes you invincible, then things naturally fall into place for you.

The downside was that whenever anyone *did* have the misfortune to make a colossally bad decision, and this only happened once every couple of generations or so, it created quite the scandal, and the offender was treated pretty much as if they'd committed murder, or worse. Losing your Touch was a hangable offence in our family.

"It's not a superstition, Jilly," Xan said, looking serious for the first time that morning. "I've seen the effects of it firsthand."

"Oh, Xan, you know how sorry I am about that, but your poor parents ... anyone can make a mistake."

It had been a dark time for Xan's family and I still burned with shame when I remembered how the three Blackwood children had been treated during the tragedy. Somehow, when Xan was about twelve years old, his father had lost his *Touch*, an event which sent shockwaves of mortified outrage throughout the entire family. In the space of a year, Xan's parents had lost most of their fortune in bad investments; summer homes had to be sold off, the private jet and car collection rehomed and the children pulled from their exclusive private school in Switzerland. Finally, only their rambling old Blackwood estate and stables remained.

To top it all off their parents had been killed in a car crash shortly afterward, leaving Xan, Sally and Alastair orphaned. I'd like to say our relatives welcomed them in with open arms but it was quite the opposite. My cousins had been treated a little like lepers after that; as if their parents' bad luck might be somehow contagious.

"Well, if I can't blame them for losing everything then I can at least blame them for dying and leaving me and the twins to shoulder all their debts," Xan said, frowning. "Anyway, I'm not here to dredge up the past, Jilly. I need your help."

"Xan, I'd love to help you but I have dozens of shows coming up. I can't take time away to go on an adventure with you; Bally and I are riding our first Grand Prix tests in public this winter; we need to practice."

"Well, bring him with you. Word is that Old Ruthless has a world-class horse facility that she hoards to herself; a full-sized indoor arena, outdoor jumper ring, a galloping track, and miles of pasture. Apparently, it's horse paradise there."

"Oh, that does sound nice. But she didn't invite me, Xan; she invited you and your horse."

"Hor*ses*," Xan reminded me, "she said hor*ses;* plural. And I only have one. Anyway, it's not like she really expects me to arrive alone to her spooky old mansion. Nobody in their right mind would show up *there* without a sidekick."

There was a loud knock at the kitchen door and Gilbert pushed inside without waiting for an answer. His blond curls were tousled around his head in a halo and his cheeks were red from the frosty air outside. He held Bally's fallen halter and lead rope in one hand and his blue eyes sparkled with their usual good humour.

"Hey, Jilly," he called, "Bally made it back safe and sound. Do you know whose horse trailer…"? He stopped as soon as he saw Xan, the easy smile slipping from his face. "*Master Xander*," he said sarcastically through gritted teeth.

"Jaros," Xan said coldly, using Gilbert's last name. "Yes, that's my trailer you're wondering about and that's my horse inside it. I'll most likely be invited to stay the night so you might as well unload him. Make sure you bed his stall deeply and mind how you handle him, he's expensive and I don't want him ruined by incompetence."

"Xan stop that," I said wearily. This was the only downside to having Xan around. I constantly had to referee between him and Gil. It was practically a full-time job. "Please don't boss Gil around. He's my friend; you know that."

"I'd rather hoped you would have grown out of *that* childish fancy," Xan muttered, sending Gilbert a dark glance.

"Well, I haven't and I won't. So, you'll have to make a truce if you're going to stay the night."

Xan's eyes flashed in surprise but a second later he grinned at me and gave a little military salute.

"Whatever you say, cousin. I'm just trying to keep you from slumming with the riff-raff."

"Come on, let's go unload your horse."

I linked arms firmly with both of them and we walked down to the stable with me chattering away uncontrollably like a magpie to fill the icy silence. Nothing I said could draw more than grunts and nods out of either of them. They kept shooting glares at each other over the top of my head.

I sighed, wishing for the billionth time that they could find a way to get along. Gilbert had lived at the farm with his father, our head trainer Christoph, since he was seven years old and we'd been best friends since the first day we'd laid eyes on one another. Actually, he'd been my *only* friend back when I was a weird, scrawny kid in glasses and braids, always with my nose in a book when I wasn't on a pony.

The kids at school hadn't liked me very much, although

some of that *might* have been my fault. Not only was I the daughter of the most eccentric, rich and dangerous family in town, I was also the type of kid who corrected people's grammar and randomly shared scientific facts. Also, at that age, I was convinced that I was some sort of ghost whisperer. I thought I saw spirits everywhere and I'm sure I terrified my classmates and half the teachers on more than one occasion. By the age of six, I'd resigned myself to a life of friendless solitude except for when Xan came to visit, but when Gilbert had arrived, he'd changed everything for the better.

As long as we'd been friends, Gil and Xan had been rivals. Xan had sometimes spent the summer at Greystone and they'd competed against one another in horse shows for years before Gil decided to focus on dressage and Xan gravitated toward show jumping and eventing. Their dislike of one another hadn't faded over time; it probably didn't help that Gilbert not only had access to all Mother's amazing horses but was also a brilliant horseman who could outride Xan any day of the week, blindfolded.

I breathed a heavy sigh of relief when we finally reached the small silver truck and trailer parked in front of the east wing of the stable.

"Oh, that's not Teddy," I said, stepping up on the running board to peer inside. Instead of Xan's usual bay eventer, Teddy, a strange black horse stared back at me balefully, yanking mouthfuls of hay from his net and chewing industriously despite the small space he'd been crammed into. It was a decent enough trailer but much too small for a big horse like that. "Let's bring him out so we can see him better."

There was a brief moment where Gilbert and Xan stared each other down, each struggling not to be the one to make the first move. It was like this ridiculous silent show-down.

"Did you want me to unload him by myself?" I asked in exasperation.

That seemed to break the spell, Gilbert lowered the heavy back ramp while Xan slipped in and went to the animal's head, clipping on a lead rope.

The horse marched backward down the ramp and stood there with his head held high, surveying our stables with a commanding look. He wore an immaculate green travelling blanket monogrammed in gold thread with the Blackwood crest and his midnight black coat glistened in the morning light, not a hair out of place.

"Ooh," I said, "Xan, he's beautiful. But where did he come from? Where's Teddy?"

"Sold," Xan said quickly, not quite meeting my gaze. He knelt and busied himself taking off the horse's shipping boots. "I had to sell Teddy and all my other projects to afford this guy. Alastair found him for me, actually, and he loaned me the rest of the money to buy him."

"Alastair?" I said in surprise. Xan's brother wasn't exactly the type to go around spontaneously loaning money; he was notoriously cagey with his wallet and almost every penny they made went into maintaining their crumbling estate.

"I know what you're thinking, but he's not all bad. He's been almost human lately. I think he must have a girlfriend. He's been positively friendly."

"Oh, good," I said unenthusiastically. As much as I loved Xan, I could not bring myself to feel the same way about either Alastair or his twin sister Sally. Growing up, they'd been the sort of cousins who were always creeping around listening when they shouldn't be, or smuggling small, valuable things into their pockets, and pinching the younger children when none of the adults were watching.

"Alastair felt that it was important to make a good impression on Great Aunt Ruth when I arrived. She's not going to sponsor someone who doesn't have a great horse; she wants to see potential. A sponsorship for me would mean an injection of cash for our estate, too. It would benefit all of us."

"Of course," I said, swallowing hard. I hoped for his sake that things turned out but they were sure going through a lot of trouble over a simple invitation. It wasn't like Great Aunt Ruth had promised Xan anything other than a visit. And the casual way he'd just sold Teddy bothered me most of all.

Horses were bought and sold all the time, of course, but Teddy had been a nice horse and he'd tried so hard for Xan. I hoped he'd ended up in a good home.

"No more project horses or race-track rejects for me, cousin," Xan said, seeming to guess my train of thought. "This one is a seasoned Advanced level eventer." Xan grinned and slapped the animal's well-muscled shoulder with pride. "Jilly, meet Rigel."

"Well, he certainly is stunning," I said diplomatically, reaching out to touch the horse's proudly arched neck. Xan had always depended on buying either very young horses for cheap or retraining talented horses off the track like Teddy. He'd never had the money to buy an animal of this calibre so the least I could do was be supportive.

"Wait, Jilly!" Xan's warning came too late.

Before I could even blink, Rigel squealed, flattened his ears against his head and lunged straight toward me. There was a moment where I felt his teeth click in the air, millimetres from my outstretched arm and then his big shoulder crashed into me and I fell, landing hard on the cobblestones. I tumbled out of the way as best I could, curling quickly into a ball to protect myself from the hooves clattering dangerously close to my head.

There was a high-pitched yowling sound and suddenly I was yanked from the ground and set abruptly on my feet, a pair of strong arms wrapped protectively around my shoulders.

"Jilly," Gilbert said, peering anxiously into my face and brushing my hair out of my eyes, "Did he hurt you?"

"I ... I'm fine," I said breathlessly, leaning into him gratefully. I did a quick inventory of my body parts and found I was mostly undamaged. I gingerly rubbed my elbow where it had smacked into the cobblestones and winced.

"She'd be much better if you'd take your dirty paws off her," Xan snapped, struggling to hold his nervously prancing horse.

Gilbert stiffened but didn't let go of me. He sent a deathly glare in Xan's direction.

"I'm okay, Gil," I said, gently patting his arm.

He hovered beside me protectively for another second before stepping away.

"Xan, is Rigel always like that?" I asked cautiously, my legs still shaking a little.

"Sorry, I should have warned you that he's a bit unpredictable. We got a good discount on him because they said he had a few quirks, but it's nothing I can't iron out. Don't worry, Alastair took out an insurance policy on me just in case." He laughed at his own joke. "I've only had the horse a few days but he's never done anything like that, you must have startled him ..."

"That animal is dangerous," Gil said ominously, and I put a restraining hand on his arm. Xan had just gotten the horse after all and I liked to give every creature the benefit of the doubt. Maybe Rigel had had a difficult past.

"There, he's quieter now," Xan said. "He'll be all right. Look, that's what scared him; you have a small tiger on your foot."

"Oh, Morris," I said, bending down to gather the gigantic orange tabby protectively into my arms. "What were you doing down there? You could have been killed." I smoothed the animal's ruffled fur until he relaxed against me and began to purr, kneading his big paws against my arm.

"Well, he nearly killed *us*. I don't think Rigel is used to cats. Why don't you have a sensible pet like a dog, Jilly? I can't look at a cat without thinking that they're somehow judging me."

"Oh, you know Mother," I said with a sigh, "she hates animals that don't have a purpose. Horses are the only thing allowed around here, I'm afraid, and only if they're winning ribbons. Morris gets to stay because he's useful at hunting mice."

Gil and I sent each other a conspiratorial look. Morris was more of an overweight, pampered lap cat than a hunter and probably hadn't caught a rodent in over a decade. We carefully guarded that secret from Mother, though.

"It's a pity you don't stand up to that old battle-axe more often, Jilly. I don't understand why you let her run your life …"

"Says the man who needs a sidekick to visit his elderly great aunt," I teased, quickly changing the subject. "I'd say they're equally as intimidating."

"Hmm," he said, leading Rigel from the courtyard toward the spacious barn. "You may have a point. But seriously, don't you want to get away from here, start your own life? You used to be so adventurous."

I stiffened and sent a quick side-glance at Gil. It was something he'd asked me more than once in the last few years, and especially since awful-Frederick had dumped me so hard. The truth was that I didn't have an answer; of course, I loved Greystone and the horses, but it was something else, something stronger that kept me there. Deep down I was bone-terrified to leave.

"Why would I want to give up all this?" I said lightly, as we reached the door of the opulent stable block and were greeted by a chorus of interested neighs from inside.

The stables had been built by a distant ancestor in the same style as the house, using the massive blocks of stone that gave our estate, Greystone Manor, its name. Banks of stalls ran down one side and the aisle was big enough to drive a truck, or two, through. When my parents had inherited the place, Mother had added an indoor arena so we could train year-round, even in the cold Canadian winters. She had been quite the rider in her youth, but now she left all the riding and training to Christoph, Gil, and me. She ran the business side of the operation with an iron fist, though.

Gilbert stalked away to the barn office, saying he had paperwork to do, and Morris trotted happily after him with his tail waving in the air, leaving Xan and me to our own devices.

Rigel's hooves clopped imperiously down the wide barn aisle and he looked haughtily at the horses resting in their roomy, double-sized box stalls as if he were a king and they were loyal subjects ushering him up a red carpet to his throne.

He's beautiful, but he certainly is an arrogant horse, I thought, watching as he curled his lip in a sneer when he passed our stallion Coconut's stall. *He's not kind like Teddy was.*

The other horses watched him pass without moving forward to greet him like they usually would when a stranger arrived and Coconut moved quickly to the very back of his stall and turned his hindquarters defensively to the door.

Xan put Rigel in an empty stall a few spaces down from Bally and left him restively pulling at his hay net while I gave Xan a quick tour of the stables. He'd been there many times before but our horses were always changing as new ones were bought and sold. All but Bally, of course; he was completely mine and would live here forever.

"Who are you showing this winter?" Xan asked, eyeing the impeccably bred, well-muscled horses enviously.

"Oh," I said, struggling to sound enthusiastic, "Lark, the bay mare with the stockings, Serena the grey, Lilo the chestnut gelding with the funny blaze, Carlotta the other bay, and of course, Bally. That's enough for me."

"Please don't tell me you're complaining about having too many world-class horses to ride," Xan said, raising an eyebrow, "because I'd be happy to take some off your hands."

"No, no," I said quickly, "it's just that … well, it's not as fun when you *have* to do it. If I had my choice, I'd just ride Bally. Sometimes I just get so tired of it all."

"Well, poor you." Xan said sarcastically, "that's what you get for being so talented, I suppose."

"Oh, I'm just average," I said quickly, hurrying past his comment. Even though it was all silly superstition, it was my darkest, secret fear that *my* Golden Touch was riding and that it was only the family legacy that made me bring home piles of ribbons and not talent or hard work at all. It was a worry that often kept me up late into the night. "Gilbert's riding Coconut at Grand Prix this year, too; you should see how wonderful they're doing."

"I'm surprised your mother lets a *groom* ride her prized stallion at all," Xan muttered.

"Oh, Xan, don't," I said reprovingly. "Gilbert's a beautiful rider and Coconut likes him best. You can't expect me to help you if you keep insulting my friend."

"Fine," Xander said grudgingly, then brightened. "Does that mean you'll help me with old Ruthless?"

"Hmm, tell you what; if you can convince Mother to let me go away for a few weeks then I'll come with you. As long as I can bring Bally."

"Done," he said, grinning happily, "Cousin, you and I are going to have a brilliant vacation."

. . .

He wasn't smiling quite so hard that evening at dinner when Mother turned down his request the second he opened his mouth.

"Absolutely not, Xander," Mother snapped, "And by all means, help yourself to more of my wine. I see you've already had a second glass so what's a third, really? Young people these days have no appreciation for what things cost."

Xan put the decanter back down on the table with a thud and reached for the crystal water pitcher instead, scowling down at his plate.

"Rupert!" she added sharply, fixing my father with a gimlet stare, "that meat is too rich for you to have a second piece. Consider your blood pressure. Have some of the boiled brussel sprouts if you're still hungry. Jones, you should know better than to offer it to him."

My father looked longingly after the meat platter as it was whisked away by the stony-faced Jones and sighed heavily. I made a mental note to smuggle a plate of leftovers up to his office later. Thirty battle-worn years of marriage had drained most of the fight out of him, although he could still rebel on occasion; like when he'd spirited me away to Europe and bought Bally for me.

He looked up, saw me watching him from across the table and winked.

"Did you hear what Xander said, Rupert? That dried-up old dragon Ruth has invited him to visit and he wants to take Jilly. After the way she treated me last Christmas, the things she said to me, I don't think this family should have anything to do with her."

I looked up with interest. This was something I hadn't known about. Of course, last Christmas I'd still been reeling from the public ridicule Frederick had inflicted on me a few months earlier and I hadn't paid attention to much other than my own misery.

"Oh dear, yes, unpleasant business," Father said vaguely, sneaking a piece of bread and butter.

"She accused me of bullying my daughter, as if she should talk, the old harpy. How would she know how difficult it is to be a mother? If she had had children, they would have murdered her in her sleep."

There was a shocked silence and Xan looked at me with his eyebrows raised, his lower lip quivering as he held back laughter.

Now, this was getting interesting. Great Aunt Ruth defending me to Mother? Apparently, I should have been paying more attention.

"Cousin Viola visited Ruth's estate last year," Xan said finally, composing himself, "she took her Welsh stallion, Tuppence, and said the facilities were world-class."

"Did she now?" Mother fixed him with an outraged look. "Rupert, are you listening to this? Viola went to Dark Lady Farm last year and didn't say a word to me about it. What do you think of that?"

It was clear by her look what he was supposed to think.

"Well, my dear," Father said, clearing his throat several times, "Viola does get along with everyone. I was just about to say, though, it is Jilly's birthday coming up soon and she has been a bit down. Perhaps she'd like to have a little adventure, a vacation to take her mind off things. She does train hard; she could use a break."

"Jillian doesn't need a break," Mother snapped. "There's nothing wrong with hard work. It builds character."

"Yes, you're always right, darling. But perhaps she could do with a short rest. She is looking a little pale."

"Pale?" Mother's icy gaze snapped to my face, narrowing as she looked me over. "Nonsense, she looks perfectly fine to me."

"Yes, of course, she's doing very well under the *circumstances*."

Father raised his eyebrows and sent me another small, secretive wink.

Mother drew herself upright and her face flushed until two brilliant spots of colour stood out like fall apples on her cheeks. Father's comment was referring to *The Fredrick Incident*, as we'd come to call it. It had been Mother who'd introduced me to my one-time fiancé and had pushed me hard into the union, hoping to marry me off to someone of her choosing; in this case, the son of a well-connected old school friend. He'd been older than me and charming and, as it turned out, a complete gold-digging liar who'd only been after my supposed fortune.

Too bad I'd fallen for him hook, line, and sinker. Which had made the humiliation of discovering that he'd never even *liked* me, let alone loved me, all the more bitter.

Even though it was her policy to never apologize for anything if she could help it, I knew Mother felt guilty about the whole thing. That was why Father's comment hit her in just the right spot.

"I suppose she could do with a *short* vacation," Mother said reluctantly. "And it would be nice to see what that old biddy Ruth is up to at that mausoleum of hers. I haven't seen her estate in years. I've never met a more cantankerous old hermit."

Xan spluttered into his water glass and I kicked him hard under the table to keep him from bursting into laughter.

"Jillian," Mother said finally, fixing first Xan and then me with a hard stare. "You will go and visit your Great Aunt. But you're not allowing Ballymore to travel in that tin can of a trailer. Xander should be ashamed of himself for towing such a travesty. No, Gilbert will drive you in our trailer and see to taking care of the horses. He will be your groom."

I choked and quickly grabbed for my own water glass. Gil

was going to lose his mind when I told him that he was going to have to spend two weeks cooped up with Xander.

Xan lit up, a wide, wicked smile spreading across his face. I could just see him envisioning the good impression he'd make on Great Aunt Ruth when he showed up with a fancy trailer, his own groom, and the impeccably bred Rigel in tow.

"Good, it's settled then," Mother said, "Jillian, I'll expect a full report, complete with photos, of Dark Lady Farm when you get back."

And, just like that, my fate was sealed.

Gilbert took the news just about as well as I'd expected. "No way. Coconut has his Grand Prix debut coming up in two months. I can't afford to go on a road trip with you and that pretentious, blathering idiot."

"I'm sorry, Gil, I did try and get Mother to let Coconut come, too, but she wouldn't hear of it. And Xan's not so awful if you give him a chance. He's really funny."

"Yes, at other people's expense; I don't know why you spend time with him, Jilly."

"Well, because, besides you, he's the closest thing I have to a friend. Everyone else hates me."

"Nobody in Maplegrove hates you," Gil said with a sigh, repeating what he'd been telling me off and on for most of our lives, "they just …"

"Think I'm crazy. I know, I remember the looks people gave me after Frederick told them what I was really like."

"Nobody believed that idiot, Jilly. You have more people on your side than you think. But you have to give them a chance to know you like I do."

"Fine, whatever," I said, changing the subject quickly, "look, don't you think it will be fun going on an adventure? We can eat junk food and stay up late and explore Great Aunt

Ruth's mansion. It's probably haunted; remember how we used to go around looking for ghosts when we were kids?"

I broke off in surprise, wondering what on earth had prompted me to use the words *haunted* and *ghosts* voluntarily out loud after all this time. It was an unspoken family rule never to speak about that odd part of my past. My parents had gone to great lengths to develop me into a normal adult and we'd all agreed that my weird childhood delusions belonged firmly buried in the past.

"Yes," Gil said slowly, giving me a strange look, "you dragged me all over the countryside on your ghost-hunts and when we got into trouble, and we usually did, *I* got blamed. You sure had quite the imagination."

"Um, right," I said, twisting my hands together nervously.

The thing was, back when I was little, I hadn't been making up the stories about ghosts just to annoy my mother and terrify the local children; in my mind, I'd seen spirits as clear as day and talked to them, too. I hadn't known then that it was just a delusion, a trick of the mind, the result of an overactive imagination run wild.

I'd loved my imaginary ghosts better than real children. To me, they were clear as day and I couldn't understand why other people couldn't see them, too.

"Look, she's right there," I'd told eight-year-old Kristy Saunders who'd marched boldly over to see why I was talking to a tree on the school playground. "She wants to play with you, too."

Kristy, to her credit, had squinted hard at the shady spot under the trees where I'd pointed, toward where the little barefoot ghost-girl was turning cartwheels across the grass. Kristy had tilted her head and held her breath, trying her best to see if there was truly anything there. But the next moment her hopeful expression had fallen and she'd called me a liar and shoved me so hard that I'd skinned my hands and knees when I hit the rough ground.

That didn't stop me, though. For such a smart, bookish kid it took me an incredibly long time to learn to keep my mouth shut. By the time I'd realized that maybe some things were best not talked about, I'd developed quite the reputation as that crazy ghost kid. Kristy and her friends had called me Casper one day and that nickname had stuck until well after I'd graduated from high school. There were probably still townspeople who called me that behind my back.

Only my Scottish Nanny, and ever-loyal Gil, had at least pretended to believe me. Nanny had even encouraged me to write all my ghostly encounters down. When Mother had found my stash of carefully written ghost journals (complete with maps and illustrations), she'd been livid. "For heaven's sake, Jillian," she'd said in exasperation, "do you want this family to be a laughing stock? I'll thank you to keep your wild stories to yourself. You don't want the commoners to come after us with pitchforks and torches like they did back in the 1600s, do you?"

Things might have turned out much differently if I'd just listened to her for once.

"Jilly," Gilbert said, bringing me out of my dark thoughts, "do you really think your Great Aunt is going to let your *groom* tramp all over her mansion? I'll probably end up sleeping in the horse trailer; where the help belongs."

"No, you won't," I said firmly, although sleeping in the horse trailer was hardly a punishment. It had deluxe accommodations the size of a small house, a full kitchen, and two bedrooms. We'd spent many a horse show bunked in there. "Where I go, you go, remember? We're a team. Besides, we'll just say you're a friend of the family, or, better yet, another cousin; there's enough of us around that she won't know the difference. Xan needs my help so he'll play along."

Gilbert set his jaw in a hard line and shook his head, not meeting my eyes. "Fine. To keep you out of trouble, I'll drive you to the backwoods of Quebec so you can spy on your crazy relatives. But I won't like it."

"Oh, thank you," I said, pinning him in a tight hug, "you won't regret it, you'll see."

"I already do." He kissed the top of my head before extracting himself, then sighed and walked back into the barn.

Chapter 2

*E*arly the next morning, when the world was still sleeping and the grass was stiff with frost, we loaded Bally and Rigel in our roomy, six-horse trailer and started our road trip east. These days I rarely left Greystone except to go to horse shows and I was practically bouncing up and down on my seat with excitement, like a little kid.

"Let's have lunch at a real truck stop, Gil. I want to eat all the greasy food I can get my hands on." I hardly ever had access to junk food; training all the time under the watchful eyes of Christoph and Mother meant that I ate mostly healthy, balanced meals and protein smoothies and I hadn't had a burger in months. My mouth watered just thinking about it.

"Sure," Gil said, turning to me with an easy smile.

We drove down our long driveway and turned right onto the narrow, tree-lined road that rose and fell sharply several times before plunging down the hill into Maplegrove.

I looked out the window wistfully at the still-sleeping town. A place I hadn't visited in nearly a year. Not since Fredrick had shamed me publicly in front of the entire town.

It was a charming, picturesque village like something out

of a storybook. Wide tree-lined streets housed small, specialty shops, mostly owned by our family and rented out to enterprising locals. In another hour it would be bustling, but right now with its lightly frosted roofs and brightly painted doors, it looked like a snow globe right before it gets shaken up.

I'd spent my whole life waiting to not feel like an outsider here; to just blend in with the crowd and truly belong. If I could be one of those girls who could casually pick up a coffee at MapleBrew, call out cheerful morning greetings to all my friendly neighbours, and then maybe saunter over to the local bookstore and just browse there without anyone staring, whispering or sending me curious looks I felt my life would be perfectly complete. There had been a very short time in my life when I'd thought that fairy-tale existence was nearly in my grasp. But Frederick had ended that. He'd made sure that any hope of my fitting into this town had been destroyed. Permanently.

As a teenager, being friends with Gil had opened a lot of doors to me that normally would have been slammed in my face. Everyone in town loved him. He'd excelled at every sport our small school could throw at him and after graduation he'd been offered scholarships from a dozen good schools. Nobody could understand why he'd turned them all down to stay home to ride horses instead.

He'd been the town golden boy and more than one jealous girl had demanded why on earth he chose to hang out with *me* when he could take his pick from any girl at school. There had even been a rumour that I'd cast a spell on him.

The truth was that I didn't know why Gil stayed friends with me either. I'd been adventurous as a child but I'd turned into a cautious and shy teenager, something that had stayed with me even after graduation. I wasn't particularly smart or interesting and my social skills were clumsy at best. I was pretty enough in my own way but I practically lived in riding clothes and rarely bothered with make-up or to let my hair out of a ponytail.

I'd been shocked when awful-Frederick had shown up and swept me off my feet. Honestly, there'd been a small part of me that had been relieved when he'd turned out to be a gold-digging liar; at least that had explained his baffling interest in me in the first place.

I sighed heavily and Gil, guessing my thoughts, reached out to squeeze my hand. "We could stop here first if you want. You might remember that MapleBrew makes the world's best cinnamon buns. See, it even says so right on the sign."

"No, that's okay," I said lightly, my mouth watering at the memory of those sugar-glazed cinnamon buns that were a local specialty. "I had the new groom, Andre, pick us up some snacks." I held up the bag of tantalizing road-trip junk food that I'd bribed one of the grooms to smuggle us from town. "I made sure to get those awful sour candies you like, too."

"Perfect." He laughed. ``You always know the way to my heart.''

I leaned back happily in my seat with my shoulder wedged comfortably up against Gil's and firmly put all thoughts of Maplegrove behind me. I'd sandwiched myself in between Gil and Xan, mostly to stop them from fighting, but it hadn't been necessary. Xan had fallen asleep even before we'd left the drive-way, probably due to all the scotch he'd swilled down the night before when he stayed up late playing billiards with my father. That left Gilbert and me to entertain ourselves.

We hadn't had the chance to hang out together alone much this last year. I hadn't realized how much I'd missed this easy comradery.

We ate lunch as we neared the Quebec border. Gil found me the best, greasiest truck stop he could, and we sat side by side on revolving stools at the yellow, faded Formica counter and had our coffees in battered white mugs.

"Cheers," I said, clicking my mug against Gil's. "Congratulations on finding the Best. Diner. Ever."

Xan was still feeling a little ill; he'd taken one look at the menu and headed back to the truck to have bottled water and antacids, leaving Gil and me to stuff our faces in peace.

I'd ordered a dripping, pulled pork sandwich with poutine *and* coleslaw on the side, and followed it up with a gigantic slice of lemon meringue pie.

I sighed in happiness and patted my full stomach appreciatively.

"This reminds me of the old days when we'd spend the whole summer travelling to horse shows. Remember how much fun we always had?" I asked, licking a trace of sticky meringue off the edge of my thumb. My formative years had been spent travelling with Gil, Christoph, and sometimes my parents from one horse show to another, first in Canada and then down to through the States as far as Florida. That had been my whole world right up until Fredrick had appeared on the scene.

"Those were good days, Jilly," Gil said with a sigh, looking down at his plate. "Too bad they couldn't have lasted forever."

"Yeah." I sighed and then stood up abruptly with a startled yelp as the bell over the front door jangled and an icy breeze blew across the back of my neck. It felt like invisible spiders had crawled across my skin, and I involuntarily shuddered. I spun around to face the doorway, overwhelmed by the uncomfortable feeling that someone, or some*thing*, dark and malevolent was staring at me very intently. For a moment I thought I could see the dark figure of a man, arms crossed, watching me with an expression full of hatred. But the next second there was nothing there; the doorway was empty, just the bell swinging back and forth slightly in the breeze.

Just my imagination, I told myself nervously. Ever since the traumatic Frederick incident, I'd been more wound up than usual and once in a while I saw things that weren't there. Just little things like flashes in my peripheral vision or imagining that someone was standing behind me. My doctor had said that it was probably a perfectly normal stress response and that eventually it would go away on its own. I certainly hoped so. I did not need any more crazy in my life.

A heavy man dressed in plaid sat a few stools down from us at the counter and I caught him staring at me with his eyebrows raised. I smiled back weakly before sliding shamefacedly back into my seat, still rubbing my neck. My first day out in public in months and I had somehow already managed to draw attention to myself.

"Jilly, what's wrong?" Gil asked laying a steadying hand on my wrist.

"Nothing," I said quickly, wrapping my hands around my steaming coffee mug to thaw them. "It's cold in here."

Gil looked at me quizzically but didn't argue.

"Well, we'd better check on the horses again and hit the road," Gil said, standing up slowly. He looked as reluctant to go as I was. Still, we had to get moving; we had over half a day left to travel.

It was surprisingly warm outside for late fall. The sky overhead was cloudless and blue and the day had a bright, hopeful feel to it.

"Hey guys, how was your lunch?" I called to the horses as I opened the side door to the trailer. But when I stepped into the spacious living quarters, I got a surprise.

"Morris!" I scolded, seeing the fat orange tabby lying flat on his back on the plush leather couch, his front paws folded lazily over his chest. "How did you get in here?"

"Meow," he said languidly, opening one green eye and stretching out a gigantic paw in my direction.

"Well, it's too late to do anything about it now," Gil said, laughing. "We can't send him back. We'll just have to make sure he doesn't escape and get lost."

I bent down to rub the cat's furry belly, laughing as he broke into a rumbling purr.

I went through the interior door into the tack room, and then through a second door into the compartment where the horses were quietly eating their hay.

"Are you guys comfortable enough in here?" I asked, inspecting their hay nets and offering them both a good drink of water. If the trip were any longer, I'd pull them out so they could walk around and stretch their legs, but right now they looked fine. And, as wonderful as the truck stop was, it wasn't a great place to be leading a horse around.

The second leg of our trip went much faster than the first. Xan woke up when the truck rumbled to life and was in a surprisingly good mood, even making an effort not to be outwardly rude to Gil.

We made good time even after we left the main highway and turned down a series of narrow paved roads, consulting the map from time to time. Dusk was just falling as we passed up a nicely gravelled country lane lined on either side with thick maples in all their fall colours.

"We're here," Xan said happily. But his smile faded as we pulled up to a set of imposing black gates set into a high red brick wall. The top of the wall was bound tightly with ivy and the overall look was of an impenetrable fortress.

"Well, this looks cheery," Gilbert said, staring glumly out through the windshield. Ahead of us the iron gates, with their filigreed swirls and decorative spikes, were sealed tight, shackled by multiple wraps of a thick, black chain. The message was clear: Keep Out.

Xan rubbed his finger on the side of his nose, a habit he had when he was nervous or trying to talk his way out of trouble.

"It doesn't look very inviting, does it?" I said doubtfully, peering out the window. "Are you certain she knew we were coming this afternoon, Xan? What did she say when you called her?"

"Well," Xan said, shifting around uncomfortably. Colour flamed his cheeks. "I didn't exactly speak to her directly. I meant to call last night, but I guess it slipped my mind."

"Oh, Xan," I said in dismay. "She won't know what time we're arriving. And we've brought the horses all this way."

"No fear," he said, throwing the door open and jumping out. "I'll have this sorted out in a minute. I'll call her right now and let her know we've arrived. I'm sure she's expecting me; she sent me the letter, after all."

"This is just great," Gilbert muttered at Xan's retreating back. He turned off the ignition and stared moodily up at the huge black metal sign set into the red brick wall. It showed a rearing horse and the farm name, Dark Lady Farm, in thick, gold lettering. Despite the circumstances, it was an impressive sight, especially against the autumn background of red and gold fall leaves.

I leaned forward and looked up at the sky, frowning as I saw that the bright blue had been cluttered up by dark grey clouds. The temperature had plummeted at least five degrees and it felt like it was going to snow. I fished my jacket out from the back seat and slid into it gratefully.

Out on the driveway, Xan glared down at the phone in his hand incredulously. "No cell service!" He called, looking horrified. "We are literally in the exact middle of nowhere. Unbelievable."

I slid out of the truck and stretched my cramped muscles, checking my phone to confirm that Xan was right; there wasn't any cell service.

"That's strange that there isn't a padlock," I said, looking at the heavy chain on the gate, "it must be on the other side."

"Let me check." Xan stuck his hand through the bars but they were too close together; he couldn't get in further than his wrist. He kicked the gate a few times to vent his feelings and then stopped and peered into the woods. "Here," he called, "there's a path and it looks well used. I'm going to follow it. It's sure to lead somewhere. Come on, cousin."

"Oh, no you don't," Gilbert said, appearing beside me and clamping a restraining hand around my wrist. "You're not tramping off in unfamiliar woods by yourself after that idiot. There could be wild animals."

"What?" I said in surprise. I looked down to where he gripped my arm. Gil could be overprotective at times, he'd spent a lifetime defending me from my mother and hostile townsfolk after all, but he didn't usually go around manhandling me.

I hesitated. Since my early teens, I'd made it my policy to just not bother arguing with people unless it was a life-or-death situation. It was just so much easier to give in rather than fight. And, since I'd spent my entire childhood being feisty and reckless, not having to fight for things anymore had been quite the relief.

I was on the brink of following Gil obediently back to the truck when another of those icy, wintery breezes blew over me, pulling sharply at my hair with cold, little pinching fingers. I jerked backward, tugging my arm out of his grip and looked around in surprise but the wind had gone as quickly as it had come; even the trees were still. But my passive mood had disappeared with it too.

"Gil, what's wrong with you?" I asked, rubbing the spot on my wrist where his fingers had dug in. "I think I can manage a short walk in the woods without getting eaten. You stay here and watch the horses; I'll be right back."

My voice came out sharper than I'd intended and I saw him flinch away.

"Yes, of course, *madam*," he said, clenching his jaw, "whatever her majesty orders. Please, be my guest and march right into danger like you always do."

"Fine, I *will*," I snapped, feeling my cheeks flush with heat. Without looking back, I stalked off into the woods after Xan.

"If he were my groom, I'd fire him fast, no matter how good a rider he was," Xan said loudly over his shoulder, obviously intending Gil to hear.

"He's not a groom, Xan," I said quietly, already regretting my spark of anger, "he's assistant trainer to Christoph. Or he would be if Mother would pay him full wages. Anyway, let's just focus on finding a way in."

The path was well beaten down and we found our entrance less than a hundred feet away, set deep in the stone wall. It was a smaller metal gate, just big enough for a person on foot or riding a horse to pass through. It was partially buried beneath a thick screen of ivy and was nearly impossible to see unless you were right on top of it. But it was clear someone had used it recently—there was a trodden-down pathway right through it. The door opened a good foot when Xan gave it a hard pull before getting stuck on the overhanging ivy.

"It doesn't make much sense to have a massive chain on the gate when this door is so easy to get through," I said, frowning. "I wonder why it's unlocked."

"Who cares," Xan said, flicking at a hanging strand of ivy. "It's our way in. Come on."

We squeezed through the barrier and headed between the trees, back in the direction of the main gate. But when we finally reached it, we were disappointed; a giant padlock held the loops of chain firmly together.

Gilbert leaned against the hood of the truck on the other side of the gate, arms crossed over his chest in a superior sort of way. "How did your little exploration work for you?" he said, raising an eyebrow.

"We have it all perfectly under control," Xander snapped. "No thanks to you. We'll just have to unload the horses and ride up to the house and let them know that we're here. The *groom*, of course, will have to walk. Hope you don't mind carrying the luggage, Gilbert."

Gil just shook his head and turned back to the trailer while the two of us retraced our steps toward the smaller gate. It took both our efforts, and a lot of torn ivy, to pull it open wide enough to fit a horse through but finally, it broke free.

"Look Jilly," Xan said as we paused for breath, "I know you like spending time with that brooding oaf, but it isn't healthy. You need to get out and meet real people. Socialize a little with people who are your equals. Maybe then you can finally stop moping around thinking about Fredri—"

"Could we not talk about this right now?" I said quickly. "It's water under the bridge; Frederick is long gone and forgotten. I barely even remember what he looked like."

"Hmm," Xan said, "it sure *sounds* like you're over it. Well, let me know when you're ready to start meeting real people again. I mean, if Alastair can somehow find love, then surely you can, too."

"Thanks," I said dryly. "I'll let you know."

We finally made it back to the trailer. Gil had backed the rig up a few feet and moved it to the side so it wasn't completely blocking the gate. He led Bally down the ramp just as we arrived. Bally's hooves swooshed through the thick gravel on the driveway; he nickered when he saw me and looked around in interest at his new surroundings.

"Hello, sweetheart," I said to him, coming up to take his lead rope and run a hand down his silky neck. "Should we go on an adventure?"

"This is a bad idea," Gilbert grumbled, pulling off Bally's black and gold travelling blanket that was stamped boldly with our farm name. He handed it to me and reached down to remove the matching shipping boots, running an expert hand down each leg to make sure there wasn't any heat or swelling after the long journey.

"It should be fine, Gil. We're just going to ride up to the house and see if Great Aunt Ruth is there. As soon as she knows we've arrived then we'll have someone drive us back down here, open the gate, and bring the trailer inside. It should be simple."

"Hmph," he snorted. "I don't think anything's ever simple with *you* around."

I looked away quickly, feeling strangely stung by his offhand comment. I knew he was only teasing, and he was just grumpy to be playing the role of Xan's groom, but for some reason my nose prickled, and my eyes welled with tears.

Gil looked up instinctively, eyes widening in surprise and then concern. "Hey, Jilly, I didn't mean—"

Just then Rigel skittered backward off the trailer with a rapid clatter of hooves, dragging Xan behind him. He held his head high, staring around the forest indignantly, and let out a loud, bugling neigh.

"Easy there," Xan commanded, gritting his teeth while Rigel snorted and danced around him in circles, lifting his black legs up and down in a steady march as if he were a wind-up horse on springs. He hardly stood still long enough for Xan to take his sheet and travelling boots off, and I couldn't see how we'd get manage to get his saddle and bridle on.

In the end, Gil had to put Rigel's bridle on and then hold tight to both reins to avoid being bitten while Xan quickly dressed Rigel in a red quilted saddle pad and slipped a new-looking saddle into place. There was a tense moment while he tried to tighten the girth. Rigel spun in circles, snapping at everyone within reach but finally, the horse was ready.

"Hold him still," Xan barked. He somehow managed to clamber aboard, his face flushed with anger and embarrassment. He yanked hard on Rigel's reins as he spun the horse back toward the trail. Rigel obeyed instantly but instead of rewarding him, Xan dug his spurs sharply into the horse's side several times and then cracked him two good hits with the whip, snarling angrily when Rigel bolted a few feet to one side in response.

That was a mistake, I thought, *a horse like that never forgets when you've treated them unfairly. And Rigel looks like the type to hold a grudge.*

Gil's amused smile slipped from his face and he turned abruptly away. I knew how much he hated when horses were roughly treated, even one like Rigel.

"Do you want to wait here, Gil?" I asked, gently. "We shouldn't be too long."

"Oh no, I'm coming with you. There's no way you're going off into the woods unsupervised with that idiot." Gilbert hefted his heavy backpack over one shoulder and motioned me to go ahead.

Bally calmly followed the leaping, skittering Rigel down the trail and Gil stayed right beside us, easily keeping up with Bally's leisurely pace. When we came to the little door in the ivy Rigel planted his feet, blowing and snorting at the opening and refusing to move no matter how much Xander urged him on.

"Is he always like this, Xan?" I asked, frowning as the big horse reared up in defiance then slammed his front feet back to earth.

"I have no idea," Xan said, his face flushed with rage, "this is only the second time I've ridden him. Don't worry, I'll soon show him who's boss."

Xan took one hand off the reins and raised his whip, but before he could strike, Rigel made a great leap forward and plunged through the gate at a gallop, heading into the woods with his neck braced and his nose straight up in the air, carrying Xan along with him.

"Rigel, you idiot," Xander shouted, flattening himself low over the horse's neck as tree branches snapped over his head. Grabbing the right rein in both hands and pulling hard, he managed to somehow slow the horse down and turn him, with difficulty, back onto the driveway.

"Xan! Do you need help?"

"Of course not," he snapped. "I've got this."

I eyed the nervously prancing horse uncertainly. He looked like a powder keg ready to explode.

Xan must have thought the same thing. "He just needs to blow off some steam. I'm going to let him stretch his legs a bit. I'll meet you at the house." Before I could argue, Xan loosened his grip on the reins and, without hesitating, Rigel launched up the driveway like a rocket. There was a moment where it looked like Xan might actually have things under control and then Rigel swerved and plunged into the nearby woods.

"Xan!" I called, standing up in my stirrups to see the driveway better.

"I'll meet you theerrrrre," Xan's voice drifted back through the woods.

"It's okay, Bally," I said, reaching down to pet the grey horse's shoulder. He raised his head slightly and blinked a few times as if trying to comprehend what had just happened, and then he dropped his head with a sigh and reached out to nibble at some grass at the side of the trail.

"I'm not sure that Bally is even a real horse," Gil said, laughing. "Nothing much fazes him, does it?"

"That's because he's perfect," I reminded him. "I hope Rigel doesn't get hurt with all that galloping. He just spent the whole day standing in the trailer; it can't be good for his legs to take off without even a warm-up."

Gilbert chuckled under his breath. "I don't think an animal that awful will hurt himself; he looks like the type that will live forever."

"Well, Xan can't exactly afford to replace him if he gets hurt. Should we try to follow them or keep heading toward the house?"

"House," Gil said without hesitation. "Xan's a somewhat decent rider; he can take care of himself and honestly, he deserves what he gets. I'm sure he'll meet us back at the driveway soon."

"All right," I agreed, looking anxiously into the woods. Xan *was* a brave rider and he was used to eventing and hunting, after all. A gallop through the forest *should* turn out okay. Maybe.

The temperature dropped again and I shivered, wishing I'd brought winter gloves; my thin leather deerskin ones didn't do much to keep out the cold. The dark clouds sat low over our heads, threatening snow, and I tilted my head back, marvelling at the contrast between the steel grey sky and the magnificent gold and red bursts of maple leaves towering over us.

Bally stepped lightly along the driveway, looking around with interest and snorting softly under his breath with each step. His short, grey mane bounced up and down on his neck as he strode along.

Gil walked silently beside us, easily matching Bally's pace and though he didn't say anything, I could sense the tension fading away from him. Gil was different when it was just him and me; that defensive attitude he put up around the rest of my family fell away and he was his usual funny old self again.

"Come on, admit it," I said, smiling down playfully at him, "this is more interesting than training all day long at home. It's an adventure."

"You and your adventures. Remember the time you convinced me there was a ghost in the machine shed? We had traps set up everywhere."

"I think we caught Christoph instead," I laughed, surprised

at how good it felt to talk about this stuff again after all this time. I'd almost forgotten how much fun we'd had as kids.

"Uh-huh, and the time we were biking home and you decided to try a new shortcut, and we ended up lost and the police had to bring us home."

"Oh, jeesh, Gil, you only remember the times things go wrong—"

"Like the time we nearly drowned in the river."

I sucked in my breath and looked away, not meeting his questioning gaze.

"Jilly?" he asked uncertainly. "Are you okay? I'm sorry, I wasn't thinking. I forgot about what happened afterward."

I shivered, no longer seeing Bally or Gil or the surrounding woods as the memories rushed over me.

The last summer that I ever saw the ghosts, when I was fourteen years old, I'd heard a child calling out for help from the middle of the Greystone River. Gil couldn't see or hear him of course, but the child's cries had driven me frantic. I couldn't just ignore them so I'd jumped into the river and Gil had followed after me like the good friend he was. We were both good swimmers but we'd nearly drowned that day and no amount of explaining or apologizing from me could appease my parents and Christoph.

I'd been grounded, banned from seeing Gil, and forced into an intense month of sessions with a creepy child psychologist who'd made me cry when he relentlessly tried to make me see how illogical my ghost obsession was. Worst of all, despite my hysterical begging, Nanny, who I'd loved like a real mother, had been fired, banished to who knows where and never heard from again.

"You'll get over it," Mother had said coldly when I'd collapsed into a frantic fit of sobbing. "You're fourteen years old, Jillian. You're much too old to have a nanny, especially a superstitious old goat like that who encourages you in your ridiculous obsessions. Maybe now you'll learn to put aside your childish stories and act like an adult."

That therapy-worthy trauma had caused me to fall quite ill, so sick that for a while there was some worry that I wouldn't recover. But I did get better, at least physically, and to make me forget about Nanny, Father had whisked me away on a European vacation and bought me Bally.

Somewhere during all that upheaval, the ghosts, which had obviously been figments of an overactive imagination just like the psychologist had said, had disappeared completely. I guess it *had* helped me fit in a bit more, at least until the Frederick Incident, and having a normal-acting daughter had certainly pleased Mother. But though I'd outwardly recovered from that traumatic summer, I'd secretly felt hollow afterward, like there was a vital part of me missing. Like a spark inside had been snuffed out.

"Jilly," Gil said, sounding worried, "I shouldn't have said that … I thought that after all this time we might be able to talk about it …"

I shook my head to clear the vision and took a deep, shuddering breath.

"I'm fine. Of course we can talk about it. I just…"

But, before I could continue, the woods far up ahead of us erupted in chaos. Voices yelling, branches snapping and the sound of squealing horses and thudding hooves. There was a high-pitched, terrified human scream, and then *two* horses burst from the forest. I could barely make them out in the dying light but one of them was definitely Rigel, triumphantly rider-less with his saddle twisted to one side, and in front of him was a huge bay horse, also without a rider, who galloped away from Rigel's outstretched jaws as if his life depended on it.

Without pausing, I brushed my calves against Bally's sides and he leapt forward, launching himself up the driveway, running hard until we neared the place where the horses must have come from. I eased him to a trot, scanning the left side of the driveway for any sign of Xan. Bally slid to an abrupt halt, his ears pricking forward and his whole body rigid as he fixed his gaze on the woods to our left.

"What is it, Bally?" I asked uncertainly as he snorted and shook his head, clearly upset. This was very unlike him. Underbrush crackled next to the road and there was a low, whuffling, grunting sound that reminded me acutely of what Gil had said about wild animals roaming the woods. Just as I was about to turn Bally around and make a run for it, a massive black shape pushed itself out of the trees, gave me one long steady look out of a pair of baleful yellow eyes and shot off in the direction the horses had gone.

It was just a dog, I realized, putting a hand over my heart to steady it, *the biggest dog I've ever seen in my life.*

Bally rocked back on his heels and snorted but bravely stood his ground, watching the oversized creature lurch away up the driveway. He tossed his head and then moved abruptly toward the trees, dropping down into the woods in the direction the creature had come from.

"Bally, that's not the way," I said and then realized he was right; there was a well-used trail beneath his hooves and the leafy underbrush parted easily as we passed.

I crouched over his neck, ducking to avoid the low-hanging branches and letting him pick his own way. The trail opened abruptly into a wide clearing and Bally stopped, dropping his nose to sniff something near his feet.

"Oh, no," I said, putting a hand over my mouth.

A small, crumpled figure lay deathly still on the damp forest floor. She was around my age, dressed in knee-high leather boots, breeches, and a red knitted sweater. She wasn't wearing a helmet and her short, black hair stood up in all directions. She lay flat on the ground, head tipped to one side and one knee bent on an awkward angle. Her face was deathly white, her lips nearly blue, and I noticed that she was painfully thin with dark circles under her eyes.

Xan knelt at her side, wide-eyed and solemn. He looked like he'd hit the ground himself, one side of his jacket was covered in mud and there were leaves in his dark hair.

"Jilly," Xan said, looking up at me with serious eyes, "we need to do something."

"Is she … is she, alive?" My voice came out a squeak. I'd never seen someone lie so still.

"She's alive," Xan said, "but I don't want to move her. There was some sort of creature crashing around out here and it scared the animals. Our horses collided and both of us came off. Can you ride for help?"

"It was a huge dog," I said, "I saw it on the trail."

"Well, it was big enough that the horses probably thought it was a bear. Ride hard, Jilly. I don't know how badly she's hurt."

"Okay," I said, taking a deep breath. "I'll be as fast as I can." I turned Bally around with shaking hands and headed back up the trail. It was too narrow to go very fast but I urged him into a trot and was relieved when we finally clambered back up onto the driveway.

"Gil?" I called, standing up in my stirrups to scan both directions but there was no sign of him. I cursed myself for leaving him behind. He was going to be cranky when he caught up with us.

Bally and I cantered briskly up the seemingly endless driveway, his hooves thudding rhythmically against the ground. Dusk had fallen fast and the trees around us had taken on a strange dream-like quality; they all looked the same and I had the oddest feeling that we were cantering in place and not even moving forward at all. But finally, up ahead, there was a change in the road.

"Easy buddy," I said, drawing Bally gently to a halt. We'd

come to a spot where the driveway divided into two halves, one branching left and the other to the right. Neither direction was marked and both ways seemed equally dark and unwelcoming.

"Which way do we go, Bally?" I asked, looking at each side uncertainly. The seconds ticked by and I reluctantly directed him to the right-hand branch, hoping I'd decided correctly.

Bally stopped and tossed his nose up and down a few times, then swiveled around to look at the road behind us, nickering softly under his breath.

Hoofbeats pounded up the driveway and I turned in the saddle, expecting to see Rigel and the strange horse galloping toward me. The last thing I expected to see was a woman dressed like she'd stepped right out of those old ancestral paintings that hung in our dining room. She rode side-saddle for one thing and wore a dark cape over her emerald green dress that trailed down past her horse's knees. She looked furious as she rode up, glaring at me with a livid expression as she pulled her horse up so sharply that he sprang up on his hind legs just a few feet away from us.

"Careful," I cried, stifling a scream and laying a protective hand on Bally's mane.

But the lady didn't apologize for nearly running us over; she didn't say anything at all. She just sat there on her foaming red horse and stared at me balefully with her ice-blue eyes.

I opened my mouth to tell her about the girl hurt in the woods or at least to ask directions to the house, but my words froze on my tongue and suddenly, I felt very, very cold right down to my bones. I couldn't move, and I couldn't look away from her. Her long coppery red hair hung in bedraggled ringlets against her dark cape, bits of grass and leaves tangled in her curls. The massive black dog I'd caught a glimpse of earlier now sat on the ground behind her, a mass of shaggy black fur with only its yellow eyes and pink lolling tongue to break up the impression of darkness.

A strange prickly sensation rose up my arms and along the back of my neck, instantly making me feel ill. My stomach heaved and I would have thrown up there and then if Bally hadn't shifted beneath me impatiently, pulling me out of my trance.

I put one trembling hand on Bally's neck for support and the other hand over my mouth, fighting to stay upright.

"Beware," the woman said ominously, her voice coming out a snake-like hiss. "All ye who seek to do harm. Beware."

"P...pardon?" I said, fighting the strange lethargy that had fallen over me. I struggled to remember why I was out there, riding through the dark in the first place. "There's a girl badly hurt back there," I said with difficulty. "I need to get help, to call an ambulance. I don't know the way to the house."

All three of them, woman, horse and dog, fixed their eyes on me sternly, unmoving, as if they were part of a painting rather than real life. Then the horse lifted a foreleg and pawed the ground impatiently, tugging against the bit in its mouth. It flicked its ears forward and then flattened them back, edging sideways slightly toward Bally in a way that did not look too friendly.

The dog rose to its feet and looked up the road, whining a little under its breath.

The woman nodded curtly as if coming to a decision and suddenly, her great horse reared straight up in the air, so high it looked like it might fall over backward.

"If you are a friend then follow the path that was forbidden. If you are foe then beware my wrath. The lady rides nine," she said in a furious voice, glaring at me. She took one hand off the reins and pointed dramatically up the left side of the driveway before clapping her booted heels into the horse's side and plunging past us up the road at top speed.

"Hey!" I cried, wheeling Bally out of their path just in

time. But the trio was gone before I could even blink; there wasn't even the sound of hoofbeats left for me to follow.

I sat there, waiting for the numb, sickening feeling to pass and then shook my head to clear it.

"That was helpful, wasn't it, Bally?" I muttered under my breath. "She could have just said 'go left'."

I looked in the direction she'd chosen. Hopefully, she'd been pointing toward help and safety and not directing me to jump off a high cliff. Feeling less nauseous every second, I urged Bally back into a careful canter.

I almost cried in relief when the sprawling white Baroque-style manor came into sight. It was huge, bigger than our house at home, but it looked wild and overgrown in the dim light. Instead of the manicured front gardens back at our house, the lawn was a tangle of overgrown grass and weeds. Brambles and untamed clumps of lavender and heather grew everywhere in all directions, looking like hulking gargoyles in the failing light. The place had an abandoned look to it and I wondered if there was any help for me here at all.

"There's a light, Bally," I said. "No, there are two. One downstairs and one on the top floor. It looks like someone's home at least."

Bally dropped his head and started grazing on the sparse grass as I flung myself out of the saddle. I pulled off my helmet, set it hurriedly on a nearby stone bench, and automatically ran up my stirrups before hanging Bally's reins over a low-hanging branch.

"Stay there, buddy, I'll be right back."

Then I hurried up the stone pathway to the house.

Up close, the place looked even more abandoned. Grass covered the pathway, pushing up between the loose stones so they tripped me at every other step. The entrance was covered with fallen leaves, dirt, and a few small branches. I paused at the heavy wooden doors and took a deep breath. Now that I was here, I regretted having come so far on my own. Why hadn't I waited for Gil? Something about the house was very unsettling. Gathering my courage, I knocked hard on the door and then rang the bell.

"Hello! We need help out here! Please somebody, come quickly. There's a woman who's been hurt."

At first, there was only silence, then a sharp click sounded inside the door and I stepped back in relief, expecting it to swing open. But nothing happened.

"Hello?" I said again, trying the handle and then pressing my ear against the door. It was too thick to hear anything so I knelt next to the old copper flap for the postman to stick mail inside and lifted it carefully.

"Who is she?" someone said, in a rough, guttural voice that was thickly accented. "She must be one of *them*. We can't let her in; she'll ruin everything."

"But what can we do?" a second voice said. "Oh, I wish Estelle was back, she'd know what to say."

"Don't worry, I'll take care of this," the first voice said gruffly.

I'd heard enough. All I needed was to use their phone. Surely, that couldn't be too much trouble. "Help," I called, standing up and banging determinedly with both fists against the heavy wood. "I know you're in there. There's a woman hurt who needs an ambulance. Please help."

This time the door swung open so quickly that I lost my balance completely and stumbled inside. Before I could react, something struck me hard upside the head, and I pitched forward with a startled cry. There was no time to defend myself; the ground rushed up to meet me and all the breath left my body as I slammed into a marble entryway.

The rest was a blur as I slid in and out of consciousness; there was pain and noise and the feeling of being carried somewhere. Strange images swirled around me but whether they were real or figments of my imagination I couldn't tell. Xan's anxious face hovered into view, and then he was replaced by an image of that creepy psychologist of my childhood who'd banished the ghosts, and then it was Gil's pale face looking down at me. A dark, malevolent shadow replaced him, and I felt a stab of panic but just as swiftly it was gone. Somewhere outside a horse neighed and then a dog bayed. There was a sharp prickling sensation in my skull and then I thankfully fell into a long, dreamless sleep.

Chapter 3

When I opened my eyes again, feeling deliciously rested, I stretched luxuriously, reaching out to trail my fingers through the soft rays of morning sunshine streaming across my bed. A fire crackled comfortably in the hearth, and from somewhere came the faint, welcoming smell of rich coffee. I was toasty warm under the thick, red duvet and there was a strange, soothing, humming noise right next to my ear.

Mmm. I turned my head and nearly jumped out of my skin when I found a pair of bright green eyes peering into mine about an inch away from my face.

"Morris!" I said as the big orange cat reached out and patted my nose gently with a furry front paw. "What are you doing in the house? Mother will throw a fit ..."

I stopped and frowned, realizing something wasn't quite right; I wasn't in my own bed at all. I sat up abruptly which, it turned out, was a very big mistake. The second I moved, a stabbing pain began in my head; sort of like a jackhammer working away from somewhere behind my eyes. I groaned and squeezed my eyes shut, sliding back under the covers. I hardly dared to breathe until the pain subsided. Gradually the stabbing eased and was replaced by a dull ache.

Cautiously, I opened one eye again, staring around the room in confusion. No, I most definitely wasn't at home. I was in the middle of a comfortable, oversized, canopy bed tucked underneath a heavy red and gold brocade comforter. The dark hardwood floor was scattered liberally with multi-hued Persian rugs. A large picture window with a built-in seat took up almost the whole wall opposite. The curtains had been pulled partially open and the morning was full of sunlight. Not far from where I lay, a crackling fire danced away in a large stone fireplace.

"Where am I?" I said aloud in bewilderment. If I'd been kidnapped then they'd certainly taken some care to make sure I was comfortable. I lifted the covers and glanced down to find I was wearing some sort of awful old-fashioned white nightgown with a high lace collar and puffed sleeves.

Morris blinked at me twice, as if questioning my fashion choice, and began studiously washing his paws one at a time.

I gingerly sat up, moving inch by slow inch, trying hard not to make any sudden moves.

"Ow," I said, wincing and clutching my head. When the room stopped spinning again, I carefully felt around with my fingers to find the spot that hurt. *What the hell?* My head was padded by a thick gauze bandage that ran from the crown all the way down to the back of my ear.

There was a light knock at the door and I groaned at even that gentle sound.

"Oh dear, you shouldn't be up yet." A pretty young blonde woman with clear blue eyes and pale, almost translucent, skin strode inside. She wore an old-fashioned maid's uniform of a crisp blue dress and a white apron. She stared down at me, eyes glittering with a mixture of concern and curiosity.

"I'm Aimee," she said to me slowly as if she were speaking to a very small child. She had a strong, lilted French accent but

I could understand her perfectly. "I work for Miss Ruth. I've brought your breakfast. Don't go anywhere."

I closed my eyes gratefully and waited for the throbbing to stop. There was zero chance of me wanting to go anywhere in the next century. I felt like I'd been run over by a truck.

Her footsteps left the room and then came back, this time accompanied by the sound of wheels bumping across the uneven floor.

I peeked and saw her carefully pushing an ornate silver trolley, laden with a teapot and what looked like breakfast, across the obstacle course of carpets. The wheels jammed on an especially fluffy rug and finally, she gave up and lifted the whole trolley with a surprising show of strength for someone so tiny and set it down beside the bed with a clatter.

"You had quite the fall from your horse last night," she said breathlessly, flashing me a quick smile. "Everyone was worried about you."

"Fall?" I said in surprise, struggling to remember. I'd never fallen off Bally in my life. But there was a first time for everything and the events of last night *were* very foggy. I wasn't even sure where I was.

"That handsome man out in the hall will be glad you're awake. He didn't leave your side all night and it was all I could do to convince him to have some breakfast and a rest. He's been that anxious."

"Fredrick?" I said, in confusion. And then instantly regretted my mistake. Of course, no loving fiancé was worrying about me in the other room. Even when we'd been together, Fredrick had never *really* felt anything for me other than contempt. He'd been a wonderful actor, though; I'd thought he'd loved me the whole bloody time.

Pain was a funny thing, because, whenever I felt like I was completely over my ex-fiancé, a moment like this would happen and the terrible agony of watching him saunter away from our disastrous engagement party without a backward glance would hit me all over again.

"Fredrick?" Aimee repeated in surprise. "Well, I thought his name was Gilbert, but I could have misunderstood."

"No, no, you didn't," I said quickly. "Of course, it's Gil, he's my best friend."

"Oh, is that what they're calling it these days?" she said archly. "The way he looks at you says a little more than a friend. I know a thing or two about love."

"Do you?" I asked faintly, avoiding any talk of me and Gil like the plague. When I was growing up *everyone* except Mother had assumed that we'd eventually become a couple. But honestly, I loved him too much for that. The fear of messing things up and losing him completely was stronger than anything else. I'd never risk it in a million years. "Are you seeing someone special then?"

"Oh yes," she said, her eyes sparkling, "he lives in town and he's brilliant, sophisticated and handsome … and oh, well, just everything. I don't know what I'd do without him."

"Well, it sounds like he's lucky to have you, too."

"I'm the lucky one. He could have any girl he wanted but he chose me."

I winced at the familiar star-struck look in her eyes. After Frederick, I'd vowed that I'd never fall for anyone that hard again. I hoped for her sake that her boyfriend was just as crazy over her as she was of him.

"I don't remember anything at all about last night," I said, changing the subject. "Is Bally okay?"

"Is that your horse? Of course, he's fine; he's tucked away in the stable snug as a bug. Doctor Crane fixed you up but he did warn us you might have some memory loss. We'll let you rest and then tomorrow we'll get you packed up and sent back home to your family safe and sound."

"Doctor Crane?" I said in alarm, nearly sitting up before I

remembered how much that hurt. "Ow, oh, sorry. It's just that name; I knew a Doctor Crane when I was a child."

"It is a bit of a strange name, isn't it? He looks a bit like a crane, or a stork, too. He's an odd bird but he's nice enough and good at his job. He's served as the family doctor here for years, I'm told. As did his father before him."

I lay back on the pillow, biting the inside of my cheek anxiously. Of course, this wouldn't be the same Doctor Crane. The surly, impatient one I'd been forced to visit had been a child psychologist, not a family physician. They couldn't be the same man.

"Do you know if he has a brother?" I asked cautiously.

"Well, I really wouldn't know. I only see him when he visits your Aunt Ruth and then he's not exactly very social."

"Is that where I am?" I asked tentatively. "At Great Aunt Ruth's?"

"Did you hit your head that badly?" Aimee said with a startled look. She turned toward the fireplace and knelt to toss another log onto the crackling fire, making the sparks hiss and fly up the chimney. "You're at Dark Lady Farm, of course; your cousin said that you all came to visit Ruth."

She shot me a quick, sideways look. "Of course, there must have been a misunderstanding because Ruth left on holiday and won't be back for another month. You must come again in springtime, though. Dark Lady Farm is beautiful in the spring."

I squinted at her, confused, struggling to think. I remembered Xan showing up at Greystone with a letter and then some galloping and then nothing but darkness.

An icy draft blew down the hallway, throwing my bedroom door open against the wall with a bang and then slamming it shut again.

"Ooh, that wind," Aimee said with a gasp. "It just comes rushing inside whenever the doors or windows are open. It's been worse than ever these last two weeks ever since …" she stopped abruptly, "Ever since that big storm we had."

I was only half-listening to her. I kept my eyes shut tight and clutched my throbbing head with both hands, waiting for the pain from the banging door to subside again. But, behind my closed eyes, instead of darkness, I saw a series of disjointed pictures; memories playing inside my mind like a movie. Mother's disapproving stare, Xan eating eggs in the kitchen, driving in the early morning sunshine leaning companionably against Gil, Bally running, a black dog growling in the darkness …

I opened my eyes again abruptly to find Aimee watching me, the open, friendly expression she'd worn earlier replaced by a deep frown.

"I think I remember something," I said, rubbing my temples.

"Do you? Well, that's good. The doctor will be pleased." Aimee leaned forward to lift a black, metal poker from a rack beside the fireplace and gave the coals in the fire a violent stir.

"Yes, Great Aunt Ruth sent my cousin Xan a letter asking us to come."

"Did she now? Well, that's strange. What else do you remember?" Aimee stood up slowly, gripping the poker tightly in both hands, and turned to face me, the smile on her face not quite reaching her eyes.

"We were riding in the woods and there was a strange horse … more than one maybe … Xan was on the ground and there was a girl who was hurt … oh, I was supposed to ride for help."

I struggled to sit up; certain that I'd failed in my mission to get help and had left everyone in the woods to freeze to death while I was lying safe here in bed.

"Now, now." Aimee's expression was sweet concern again. She hung the poker up and hurried to my bedside. "Everyone is just fine. Your companions are fit as fiddles, other than being worried about you. The doctor says just one more day of rest and then you'll be safe to travel back home to your own bed. I expect you'll want to leave first thing tomorrow."

"But the girl who was hurt—"

"Don't you worry about Estelle. She had a bit of a tumble off one of the horses just like the rest of you. Which just proves my theory that horses are terrible, unpredictable beasts that humans have no business riding. I honestly don't know what anyone sees in them. But anyway, she's had a bad sprain and a knock on the head, but she'll be right as rain in no time."

I sank back into my pillow, exhausted. The events of yesterday and last night came flooding back, but the pieces were all jumbled together, and I couldn't tell what had been a dream and what was real. I remembered bits of our trip out here; there was the truck stop and some good poutine (the kind you can only hope to get in Quebec), and then riding Bally through the darkening woods. After that everything was all muddled up.

"I'm very confused," I said finally. "You said Great Aunt Ruth has gone away? She invited us, well, Xan anyway, to come to stay with her."

"Oh dear, no, I'm sorry, Ruth is in, um …" she hesitated and bit her lip "… Florida, looking at horses. She'll be gone for over a month. What a pity you missed her. She didn't mention anything about having guests. It must feel a bit embarrassing for you showing up here in the night without an invitation; I suppose you'll want to be on your way first thing in the morning to save everyone any more trouble."

I sighed in frustration, wondering why on earth I'd trusted Xan to make sure things were organized. Who knew if my cousin had answered Great Aunt Ruth at all when he received the letter? Perhaps she'd just given up on him coming at all and had made other plans.

Morris batted me gently on the arm with his big paw. I

reached over absently to pet him and, in doing so, happened to glance up at the painting hanging directly to the right of my bed.

"Oh," I said, scooting backward in alarm, "she was in my dream last night."

It wasn't exactly the type of relaxing artwork meant to be hanging in a bedroom; a woman on a rearing blood-red horse stared out from the canvas with an outraged expression on her face, one raised hand bearing an outstretched dagger as if she were about to stab anyone who looked at her.

"Oh, *her*," Aimee said, looking at the painting distastefully. "The Dark Lady. She's everywhere around here. A bit of an obsession with the locals."

"I wonder how I dreamt about her? I was galloping on Bally and I came to a crossroads. That lady in the emerald dress showed me the way to the house. She said something strange, too, something about a lady riding nine horses or something. And her eyes were so piercing, she acted almost as if she hated me at first; isn't it funny how dreams can seem so real sometimes?"

Aimee cried out sharply and I turned to look just as the half-filled coffee cup in her hand crashed to the stone floor, shattering into a million pieces.

I clutched my head and shut my eyes tight to block out the painfully sharp clatter. It didn't work.

"How clumsy of me," Aimee said in an unnaturally high-pitched voice.

I squinted one eye open to find her kneeling beside my bed, her face burning bright red as she used the metal-handled broom and dustpan from the fireplace to hastily sweep up the mess. "I've ruined your coffee. You stay right there and I'll get you a new cup."

"That's all right, I don't need—"

"Nonsense, I'll be right back."

With that, she rushed from the room.

"What was that all about, Morris?" I asked, scratching the soft ridges between his ears. "Things are certainly strange here so far. Mother will be pleased to know *that* anyway. I'd better remember to write everything down."

"Meow," Morris said. He sniffed the air inquisitively and then reached a furry paw across me in the direction of the covered serving dish.

"Do you want to share?" I asked, pulling myself carefully upright and lifting the lid off the platter. Underneath was toast with butter and jam, perfectly fried eggs, shredded potatoes, and a woven raft of bacon. A group of miniature watermelons that had been carved to look like delicate roses sat off to one side and I held one up to inspect it.

"They must have a good cook here, Morris. Our Betty couldn't have made a nicer breakfast." I pinched off a tiny piece of bacon for him and then happily began stuffing my face, forgetting everything but the food in front of me.

A small noise made me stop eating and look toward the door. "Gil!" I said delightedly, "I'm so glad to see you."

My voice faltered as I took in his hard expression and crossed arms. He looked two parts relieved and one part very, very angry.

"Are you okay?" I said uncertainly.

In two seconds, he'd crossed to the bed and grabbed me in a crushing hug that nearly made me drop my bacon. My head throbbed and my whole body felt bruised to a pulp but I just sat there in astonishment, listening to his erratically thudding heartbeat, until he pushed me away.

"I thought you were dead," he said flatly. His hand tightened on my shoulder and I yelped; I was probably black and blue all over from my fall. He jerked his hand back as if he'd been stung and looked down at me anxiously. "Jilly, you could have been killed. Don't ever, ever run off like that again. I didn't know how to find you. I took a wrong path and wandered for hours."

"Gil, I'm so sorry you worried; of course I'm fine. Aimee said I just fell off Bally somehow, that's all. I must have hit my head. I'm sorry that I left you behind, though; that was stupid of me. Sit down and share some of my breakfast and tell me what happened. How did Morris get in here?"

"He insisted on coming." Gil's mouth softened into a slight smile. He sat down on the edge of the bed and lifted a piece of toast off the tray. "I took a wrong fork in the road and ended up at the back of the property somehow. There's a huge ravine there and we're lucky nobody fell in when we were blundering around in the dark. Anyway, when I finally made it to the house all the drama was already over. You and Estelle, the rider Xan found, had already been patched up and put to bed. Apparently, your great aunt has a private doctor on call and he fixed all three of you up. I think you both should have gone right to the hospital honestly. We'll have to make sure you get looked at properly as soon as we get home, you could very well have a serious concussion. And the worst of it is that, before they found your luggage, somebody dressed you in that awful nightgown."

He raised his eyebrows and gave the frilly ruffle around my wrist flick with his finger, making me laugh.

"It's terrible, isn't it?" I grinned, looking down at myself.

"Hideous. Anyway, I put Bally in an empty stall in the barn along with Rigel and the other horse. The housekeeper drove me down to the gate and I brought the trailer back up here. Morris wouldn't stay in the trailer no matter what I said; he was determined to follow me back to the house. He insisted on finding you."

He took another bite of toast and then reached out to take a sip of my orange juice before setting it down abruptly and making a face. "Ugh, this is awful. It's that organic stuff, isn't it?"

"Mmm, I don't know." I took the glass from him and took a big gulp and then another. "It tastes fine to me. It's bitter but I think that means it's healthier for you."

"Figures," Gil said, reaching out gently to tuck a loose strand of hair behind my ear. "Look, Jilly, I didn't mean to sound angry earlier. Sometimes it just feels like a full-time job trying to keep you safe."

"But you don't *have* to keep me safe," I said, frowning. "I'm sick of everyone treating me like I'm made out of fragile porcelain. I'm a grown adult. I'm perfectly capable of taking care of myself."

"Sure, you are." He *might* have meant it to sound encouraging but the words came out sarcastic as heck and I felt my temper rising.

"Fine, Gil. You've seen for yourself that I'm alive and well. You don't have to trouble yourself with my welfare anymore. That will be all; I'll see you after breakfast."

I said this as dismissively as I could, sounding uncomfortably like my mother, and the words had their effect. He drew himself away from me and stood up abruptly.

"As her majesty wishes," he said, his lips tightening into a thin, angry line. "I'll be in the barn where I belong tending to the horses."

"Good," I said to his retreating back, "stay there."

My temper faded as soon as he was gone, leaving me feeling cold, lonely and acutely aware of the ache in my head. Why was I snapping at him for no reason? It was like my equilibrium had been thrown off in the last few months. I'd spent the last six years being this mild pushover and now the closer I got to my birthday, the crankier I felt. I wasn't sure what was happening to me.

I slowly finished my breakfast and then polished off the rest of the juice, wincing at the bitter layer of pulp in the bottom. There was such a thing as taking healthy too far.

"Come on, Morris," I said still feeling a bit wobbly but determined to get up and find Xan and maybe, if he was lucky, apologize to Gil. I pushed myself unsteadily out of bed and slipped my feet into a pair of fluffy blue slippers that somebody had left on the floor beside the bed.

I went and brushed my teeth, staring at my flickering reflection in the mirror. Was this oddly blurred vision a side effect of hitting my head? Maybe I did have a concussion.

I didn't bother to get dressed, my only thought now was to find Xan and make sure he and the injured girl were truly okay. I tottered out into the hall, putting one hand against the wall to steady myself. The hall seemed endlessly long, stretched out with closed doors on either side. I walked a bit further but soon had to pause and rest again.

Oh hell, I thought, leaning heavily against the wall, *I probably shouldn't have gotten out of bed so soon. I'm not going to make it much further. I'd better go back.*

By then my head was even fuzzier; I'd forgotten which direction I'd been going in the first place and had no idea how to find my room again. I made it a few more feet and then I heard Xan's voice as clear as day.

"You, there," he said in a commanding voice, "what are you doing in my room?"

I jumped, thinking for a moment that he'd meant me.

"Time to get up, whippersnapper," a harsh, grating voice said. "You've overstayed your welcome. Time to go back where you came from."

"What are you talking about?" Xan demanded. "This is *my* great aunt's home and *I* was invited. I've been nearly killed to get here. I demand to see Aunt Ruth but first I need aspirin, coffee, and toast. In that order."

"All in the kitchen, I reckon," the gruff voice said. "You'd

The Curse of The Golden Touch

best get a move on it. I'll get your groom to load the horses and get the truck started. It's time you were on your way. You have no business here."

"Look here, you incompetent fool …" The covers rustled, and I heard Xan's feet hitting the floor. "I don't think you understand who I am. I'm inclined to speak to my aunt about having you fired. Now, where is my cousin Jillian and that sullen groom of hers?"

The dizziness and nausea faded again and I was just about to step forward and announce myself when I heard Xan's startled cry.

"What the … what do you think you're doing? Let go of me."

I wobbled around the corner just in time to see a wizened, elderly man gripping the sleeve of Xander's purple silk pajamas with his gnarled old hands.

"Stop struggling, you citified buffoon," the old man bellowed. "Get dressed and then get out of this house."

I stared at the scene in astonishment, not sure if I was dreaming again or if this was happening. The older man's shaggy white hair stood up in all directions and his milky blue eyes had a wild, unhinged look to them. His mouth hung open and he glared at Xan with a look of undisguised hatred.

"Jacob!" Aimee said sharply, as she pushed past me into the room. "What are you doing in here, you crazy old coot? These people are our guests. Let go of him right now."

Jacob swung his glare toward Aimee and then reluctantly released his grip on Xan's sleeve.

"Jacob meant no harm," she told Xan reassuringly. "He's a cranky old goat and he gets a little confused sometimes. He thought you were someone else, didn't you, Jacob?"

"He tried to kill me," Xan said angrily, pointing at the old man. "When my great aunt hears about this, he'll be fired."

"Now, now, Jacob's a, er, a pensioner. It was just a misunderstanding, is all," Aimee said, her eyes narrowing at Xan.

The old man brushed past me as he strode into the hall, knocking his shoulder roughly against mine and sending me a look of pure hatred as he passed. I stumbled backward in astonishment, wondering what on earth I could have done to earn such a glare.

"I said I want him dismissed!" Xan's voice rose to a fever pitch and I abruptly changed my mind about going in to see him. When Xan was angry, he tended to take it out on anyone around him and it was best to just go away and come back once he'd calmed down. Besides, I wasn't feeling quite myself again. That fuzzy sensation was back and my head felt like it was full of cotton. And when I held my hands up to look at them, they didn't seem to belong to me at all.

The hallway had begun to stretch in the strangest way; first, the floor shifted and stretched out as if it were a million miles long, and then the walls began to quiver like Jell-O.

"Jilly? What are you doing out here?"

"Gil?" His disapproving face swam in front of me and I giggled at the way the image shimmered and rippled as if were underwater. "Why are there two of you?"

My body felt very, very heavy and the soft hall carpet looked so inviting. Maybe I could just curl up there for a few minutes and rest my eyes.

Someone muttered something and swore next to my ear and somehow, I was swept up into a pair of strong arms and found myself moving quickly down the hallway. "Ugh, don't move so fast," I said, shutting my eyes tightly. "You're making everything spin."

There was more muttering, and then I was deposited, not overly gently, into my own borrowed bed. I sank into the mattress gratefully and began to laugh. Everything seemed hilarious for some reason and I looked over at the stern painting of the lady on the horse and gave her a wink. It must have been my imagination but both she and the horse looked scandalized.

Gil's face hovered into view and his lips moved as if he were talking, but I couldn't make heads nor tails of it. I closed my eyes and chuckled under my breath.

I blinked slowly and now it was Xan staring down at me, his hair tousled and his expression irate. I had no idea how much time had passed but at least he'd changed out of those ridiculous purple pajamas.

"Jilly, you'll never believe what just happened. I was savagely attacked in my room by some senile old servant and they refuse to fire him. Aunt Ruth is away somewhere, and her servants are complete idiots.

"I think we wasted our time coming here; this shoddy old estate is almost as rundown as Blackwood, so I doubt there's spare money to sponsor me. The horses are nice enough, though. Maybe she'll give me one of those in her will. No, don't look at me like that, you know I'm only kidding. And good grief, what on earth are you wearing?"

I blinked as Xan's relentless voice worked its way into my brain.

"It's rude to insult people's ancient nightgowns," I tried to say and then the image of his face blurred and stretched, growing black fur and ears until he looked like a very large rabbit.

I began to laugh again; this had been the most interesting morning I'd had in a long time.

"Jilly, have you been drinking? Even I draw the limit at drinking before nine a.m. What's wrong with you?"

"Could you shut up for just two seconds," Gil snapped, and I jerked. I hadn't even realized he was still in the room with us. "She's obviously been drugged with something. I don't know whether to load up the horses and get us all out of here or let her work it out of her system. There's no cell service, the servants say the land-line is down which is a likely story, and I'm at a loss as to what to do."

"Don't worry, I'm just fine," I giggled, watching as rabbit-Xan twitched his nose from side to side. "Xan's a rabbit and the room is turning upside-down. Isn't that wonderful?"

"Oh, that's not good," Xan said, his usual sarcasm dropping away. "What are we supposed to do with her?"

"Nothing at all. I am so, so, *so* amazing," I said, and it was true. Every muscle in my body was flowing like water. All those hard hours spent on horseback, all the stress from Mother's relentless criticism and the tension leftover from *The Frederick Incident* melted from my limbs, leaving me feeling deliciously light and free.

Frederick, I thought as his face swam into view. I studied his beautiful features, the chiselled cheekbones, the mocking eyes, the arrogant mouth slightly pulled up on one side.

You can't hurt me anymore, I thought in surprise. All the mortifying emotions that usually went with my memories of Frederick were gone.

Then it was my old Nanny's face there, smiling down at me warmly, her face so vivid that I could almost reach out and touch her. Abruptly, that image was replaced by the stern woman in the emerald dress; her judgemental stare burning with anger.

With a whoosh, the bed I was on disappeared completely and I stood in the same long hallway I'd been in earlier. My headache was gone, and I reached up tentatively to find that my bandages were gone, too. I was, unfortunately, still dressed in that terrible nightgown and my bare feet were cold against the worn carpet.

I turned around slowly, taking in my surroundings. The hall stretched out in both directions. It was an uninspiring space; just a tight corridor lined with closed doors. The only decorations were the paintings of rather severe-looking people that lined the hall on both sides.

There was a faint, scraping noise up ahead and, when I squinted down the hall, I could see a flickering light shining at the other end. I crept toward it, reaching out to touch the maple-panelled walls to make sure I was here and not in a dream. The walls felt solid and yet, how could this *not* be a dream? Just a minute ago I'd been in my bed and now I was here. What had happened to me?

The end of the hallway opened into a massive entrance. Two imposing front doors were on my right and to the left was a wide, curved, wooden staircase carpeted down the middle with a red runner. I stopped and stared in amazement. A huge stained-glass window dominated the second-floor landing; it must have been twelve feet tall and just as wide. Light streamed through it, splashing vibrant colour down the stairs and across the floor like a waterfall.

"Reveal what is hidden," a voice whispered almost directly in my ear. I yelped and tried to spin away, but I was stuck, frozen in place, unable to even blink. My gaze was fixed on the image in the center of the glass window. The glass depicted the lady from my earlier dream, but this time she didn't look quite so violent. She was still mounted on her blood-red horse. In her hand, she held an upraised knife but her eyes, staring down at me, just looked sad.

Suddenly I wasn't at the bottom of the stairs anymore. There was a nauseating pull in the center of my stomach, the scene shifted, and I was in a dark bedroom with three people. The housekeeper Aimee was there, as was the gnarled old man I'd seen earlier in Xan's room. He was bent nearly double now and supporting himself with a thick wooden cane. There was another figure—a slim, elfin woman about my age with dark cropped hair. She had a bruise on one cheek and a funny sort of cast on one leg though she wore a pair of dark breeches as if she had just come in from riding. All three of them stared solemnly down at a bed where a fourth person lay.

"Great Aunt Ruth," I whispered, recognizing her pale face. She was as white as her sheets and her grey hair fanned around her on the pillow. She lay with her eyes tightly shut and only the light raspy breathing indicated that she was alive at all.

"I suppose we'll have to do it," the old man said grimly, shifting to hold his cane in both crooked hands.

"It's up to us now," Aimee said tearfully. She looked up sharply toward a far corner of the room that was hidden by shadows and nodded slowly as if she were agreeing with someone hidden there. I followed her gaze but didn't see a thing.

The woman in the breeches turned to look at me slowly, her eyes wide with pain. "You have to help her," she said sadly, "the Lady rides nine." Swiftly, she reached out and grabbed the cane from the old man's hands and raised it high in the air over my Great Aunt's head.

And that's when I began to scream.

I sat bolt upright in my bed, panting and clutching at the covers. The room was cold and cast in deep shadow, the only light provided by low embers on the hearth.

Just a dream, I told myself, clutching my hands together tightly, *you're here now, safe, it wasn't real.*

There was a horrible roaring, wheezing, rumbling noise from inside the room as if the walls were splitting open, and I shrank back against the headboard with a yelp of fear, my heart pounding wildly in my chest, wondering what sort of fresh hell was about to be unleashed on me next.

Oh, for heaven's sake. I thought, realizing abruptly what that awful, familiar sound was. I could just make out Gil's dim figure splayed out in an armchair near the dying fire. His long frame was too big for the chair and his head tilted on an awkward angle, mouth drooping open slightly. He inhaled with a soft wheeze and then exhaled with a mighty, snorting roar that could have woken the dead.

That's so sweet of him to watch over me, I thought, once the sound had died away. And then he exhaled again.

"Gil," I hissed, "you're snoring. You'll wake everyone in the house up."

"Meh, schme, bleh bleh bleh," Gil muttered, still deep in sleep. He twisted around uncomfortably in the chair.

"For heaven's sake, Gil," I said, getting gingerly out of bed and tip-toeing to his side. I felt completely back to my old self again; my headache had retreated to a dull ache and I was steady on my feet. I reached out and poked Gil gently in the ribs and when that didn't work, I gave him a hard shove. "Wake up. You'll hurt yourself if you stay there. Time to go to bed."

"Wha-?" he said, looking around in confusion.

"Bed," I ordered in a whisper. "It's okay, you don't need to watch over me anymore, I'm all right now. I'm not sure where your room is, though …"

He struggled sleepily to his feet, looking bewildered, and then stumbled past me the few feet to the king-sized bed and dropped down on top of it like a mighty oak tree falling in the forest.

"No, not *there*," I hissed, giving his leg a little push, "I meant your *own* room." But it was no use; he was out cold.

I sighed heavily and tiptoed over to the fire to pile some more logs on, then went back to my side of the bed, getting under the covers and staring up at the ceiling to think about my dream again. It had been terrifying at the time, but now that I was awake and could think it through properly, it didn't make much sense.

I repressed a shiver at the memory of the helpless old woman about to be bludgeoned to death and was grateful to have the uselessly snoring Gil next to me for company.

Besides the snoring, sleeping beside Gil didn't bother me one bit. It reminded me of the good parts of my childhood. From the time we were kids, we'd travelled together to many a week-long horseshow, chaperoned by Nanny or Christoph. Our bunks in the horse trailer were side by side and we'd often staying up late to tell each other scary stories or equally horrifying jokes. We were a team and had spent as much time as possible together.

I sighed, wishing that we could both go back in time to when life was simpler, and we were just happy little kids showing ponies. Of course, childhood had not been exactly *easy* for me. But at least Gil and the horses had made it somewhat bearable.

Gil had always smoothed life's bumps for me; right up until Frederick had come into my life. That had been something even he couldn't fix for me.

I shifted uncomfortably under the covers, the memory of my mortifying engagement party, when everything had ended so dramatically, worming its way into my mind.

Mother and I had had such high expectations of the day. For once we hadn't irritated each other; we'd laughed in excitement over the preparations like we were almost *friends*. The party had been held outside in Victory Park in the center of Maplegrove. It was a beautiful wooded area that originally had been donated to the town by my parents. It had lovely gazebos and gardens and a path winding next to the river. Everyone in town had been invited to come out and celebrate. That had been Frederick's idea, of course, he was such a social butterfly and often teased me about my reclusive nature.

He'd said that he wanted everyone in town to know how wonderful I was, so he'd invited them *all* and they'd actually come, even if it was only for the free buffet. There had been music and dancing, the grassy lawn had been covered in white tents and streamers and silver balloons. It had been beautiful, and I had been happy and so, so in love.

Everyone had been unnaturally nice to me, and the afternoon and evening felt enchanted; like I was playing a starring role in some sort of fairy tale. The champagne was flowing fast and, near the end of the night, Frederick had said he needed to clear his head.

I'd waited and waited, but he didn't come back. While I sat, I noticed the funny looks people kept sending me. There were whispers. An older woman I'd never even met before came up and gave me a sympathetic pat on the shoulder. But why would she do that when I had every possible thing a person could want in life? I knew then that something was terribly wrong and that I needed to find Frederick.

It didn't take long. I hadn't searched more than a minute before I walked in on him and the perky young caterer having a "fling" right on the prep-table in the middle of the make-shift kitchen. The exquisite pain, and the utter disillusionment of that moment I'd still carried with me nearly every day since.

Worse than discovering him was the shameful memory of the hysterical outburst that had followed. I pretty much lost my ever-loving mind. I'd screamed, I'd cried, I'd sworn to forgive him and begged him not to abandon me. I'd thrown two whole trays of champagne flutes at the wall in despair. I'd wailed and torn my dress. Basically, anything desperate and mortifying a person could do, I did it. And all the while the crowd of stunned townsfolk watched in horrified fascination.

And, instead of comforting me or apologizing, Frederick had grabbed the microphone off the stage and confessed to everyone that he'd never loved me, that nobody could be expected to love a weirdo like me. And then he'd drunkenly begun listing every one of my faults, real and imagined while I stood there sobbing pathetically in a heap. The only thing that had finally shut him up was Gil's fist connecting repeatedly with his jaw.

"You were such an idiot," I told myself for the billionth time, biting the inside of my cheek hard to keep from crying at the memory of how needy and vulnerable I'd been. I would never get that image of myself out of my head.

"Not an idiot," Gil muttered, rolling over and draping an arm comfortingly across me, "schmeh bleh bah … always too good for him."

I froze for a moment, then turned my head toward him, studying his chiselled profile in the flickering firelight.

"Thank you," I whispered, but his only answer was to launch back into another round of snoring, making me laugh despite myself.

Gradually, Gil's steady breathing lulled me into a state of relaxation. He smelled like home to me; horses and hay and the woodsy soap he always used and the Italian shampoo that I'd ordered online for him to try and tame some of his curls.

I yawned and shifted closer to him, tucking myself further under his arm. Slowly my breathing fell into rhythm with his and I drifted off into a peaceful sleep.

Chapter 4

The next morning, I woke with a start to find both Gil and Morris gone and Aimee hovering shame-facedly over my bed.

The dream from last night came flooding back and I leapt away, remembering the similar way she'd loomed over Great Aunt Ruth's prone body.

"Oh, no, please don't be afraid," she said earnestly. "Your cousin Xan and that Gilbert already yelled at me, twice. I swear I didn't know how much of that medication was in your juice. The doctor just said to dissolve a tablet and that's what I did. I didn't know that stupid cook Belinda had already mixed one in, too. It was just supposed to help you sleep a little and take the edge off the pain. Not knock you out for two days. Everyone is so angry with me, but honestly, it was just an accident. Here's your breakfast and I swear, it's just food. Nothing else."

I was still groggy, so it took a minute to process all this information.

"You ... you drugged me? But why?"

"I am so, so sorry. The doctor said you needed strict rest

and he left pills for you. It was just a silly mix-up, honestly. I swear there's no harm done. How do you feel?"

"I guess I feel okay now …"

"Oh, that's good. You had no idea how worried we were. You slept like the dead: we thought you'd never wake up."

"That's an awful thought." I sat up and stretched my limbs out gingerly. Everything seemed to be in working order and, overall, I felt much better than I had the day before. "How long have I been here?"

"Two days, more or less; this is your second morning."

"Oh, poor Bally. He'll think I abandoned him."

"Jacob's been seeing to all the horses. He said that everyone's just fine. Get your breakfast and if you feel up to it later, we'll see if someone can escort you outside."

My stomach rumbled at the delicious smells coming from the breakfast trolley. Despite my mistrust of Aimee, especially after my dream last night, I was starving. And she *had* promised that my food was untainted this time. It had been an honest mistake, after all. Maybe.

"Where's Morris?" I asked.

"Who? Oh, you mean that cat? I have no idea; they're always creeping about somewhere, aren't they? I've never liked them…"

She broke off guiltily just as the door bumped open and Morris came trotting into the room.

"Meow, meow, meow," he chirped, hopping up onto the bed and marching toward me and the breakfast tray. He looked happy and well-fed; it seemed like *someone* had been taking care of him, anyway.

"There you are." I scratched him under the chin until he rumbled with happiness, kneading his big paws against the blanket.

Aimee pressed her lips into a thin, disapproving line.

"When I was growing up, it was always a rule in our house that animals should stay outside where they belonged."

I looked up at the sudden hard edge in her voice, but she was focused on arranging the coffee pot on the tray. She caught my eye and smiled. "But I guess my parents were just old-fashioned."

"They sound like my own mother actually," I said with a rueful laugh. "She doesn't believe in house pets, either."

"Huh, well those bandages on your head can come off today. They were just to keep the sutures clean."

"Sutures?" I said in surprise.

"Yes, didn't anyone tell you? You have the tiniest little cut and a bump where you hit yourself. The doctor sewed it up in two seconds flat. He said that the stitches should come out in a week or so, once it's all healed up. I expect your doctor at home can do that for you; you'll be eager to get away now that you're feeling better."

She poured my coffee and handed me the cup.

"Oh, you've hurt your arm," I said, noting the red, lumpy skin on the tender underside of her arm where her sleeve had risen.

"That's nothing." She pulled her sleeve down with a sharp tug. "It happened when I was a child."

"I'm so sorry. It was a fire?"

She turned away, her back rigid.

I've offended her, I thought with a pang of conscience.

"It was a burn, yes," she said finally, turning back to me with a sigh. "We were experimenting at home in the lab and it got out of control."

"Aimee, I'm so sorry, that's awful. Was it like a science experiment?"

"Yes, my parents were brilliant scientists. They both died in the explosion. I lived but had some burns."

"Oh my gosh, I'm so sorry," I said again, biting my lip. I never seemed to know when to stop asking questions. This was exactly the sort of reason why people didn't like me.

"It's all right," she said shortly. "It was a long time ago. Have a good breakfast."

And with that, she was gone.

"I put my foot in it that time, Morris," I said, scratching him under the chin with one hand and lifting the lid off the breakfast tray with the other. "Isn't this the strangest place, though? A spooky old mansion, an absent Aunt, eccentric staff; good thing I don't think I see ghosts anymore because this place would be riddled with them."

Morris and I made short work of breakfast, and I drained two cups of the delicious French coffee, carefully avoiding the orange juice—just in case. Now I needed to see for myself that Bally was okay.

I slid clumsily out of bed, my legs a little unsteady after all the time I'd wasted lying down. At least the pain in my head was nearly gone. My travel bag sat on an antique dresser beside a small group of horse figurines. It was still packed, and I rummaged through it to find any clothes that weren't a floor-length nightgown. I made my way to the ancient attached bathroom to have a much-needed shower.

Wow, I thought, *I don't think this place has been updated since the last century.*

The room was painted a sickly green, with a white claw-foot tub in one corner and a wooden dressing table with a built-in sink in the other. Tarnished copper pipes ran along one wall and they groaned and rattled when I turned the water on.

The shower was just a corroded metal ring above the tub that spat out an unsteady stream of water. I eyed it skeptically, but in the end, decided that even a bad shower was better than no shower at all.

Before stepping in, I stared at my reflection in the faded mirror and carefully peeled the bandage off my head, relieved that it came off easily without pulling my hair too badly.

That's not just a couple of stitches, I thought in dismay. By craning my neck at various angles, I could see at least five stitches and maybe more. The area around them was bruised and mounded up like a swollen egg I poked at the base of it skeptically, thinking that I probably should have been taken to the hospital as Gil suggested.

When I finally emerged, freshly showered, dressed, and feeling much more like myself, both Morris and the breakfast trolley were gone again. I padded to the window and looked outside, hoping to figure out exactly where the stables were.

I was in luck; my guest room was at the front corner of the house, overlooking a badly overgrown front garden and an equally untamed lawn. And beyond that was a colossal building that was the stables and indoor arena.

All right, that's more like it, I thought, eager to try out new facilities. Bally and I sometimes got a bit bored at home doing the same old routine. This might be just what we needed to add a little spark to our training.

My boots and jackets were stationed neatly beside the bedroom door and I dressed quickly, pulling on my low walnut-coloured paddock boots and a plum-coloured coat that Mother had brought back from a trip to Germany. Despite being an ogre about most things, Mother had impeccable taste in clothes; I was pretty sure she'd only had a daughter in the first place so she could dress me up like a doll. My lack of fashion sense was another constant disappointment to her. I pulled open the wooden door and looked into the hallway, trying to get my bearings.

My room was at the furthest end of a wood-panelled corridor; rows of tightly closed, polished doors lined the hall on either side. I wasn't sure which one I'd seen Xan in yesterday but it couldn't have been far from here.

Paintings of stern-faced people, most likely long-dead relatives of some sort, decorated the spaces between the doors and I couldn't help but think they were watching me disapprovingly as I walked carefully between them. Chandeliers ran the length of the hallway, shedding warm light on the rich, red carpet and intricate wood panelling.

There was no sign of anyone as I padded down the long, silent hallway, which was strange in itself. Greystone was always bustling with workers scrubbing, polishing or re-decorating under Mother's watchful eye. Especially if there were guests in the house.

I suppose we're not exactly guests here, though, I thought ruefully, *more like intruders.*

I reached the end of the hall and hesitated, staring cautiously out into the entryway. Goosebumps rose up my arms as a feeling of déjà vu washed over me and I rubbed them vigorously. I hadn't explored this far when I'd left my room yesterday and yet this part of the house was exactly like it had been in my dream.

The hallway opened into a huge foyer dominated by the massive curved wooden staircase on my left. It spiraled upward to a wide landing and then upward again to the second floor. The polished wooden steps were wide enough to drive a bus up and the dark wood had been covered in the middle with a strip of thick red carpet. The carpet was dappled with light from the window on the landing and I looked upward, knowing what I was about to see.

I froze as I gazed up at the massive stained-glass window. It was exactly like the one in my dream. A cold little shiver passed through me as I remembered the terrible nightmare that had played out in Great Aunt Ruth's room. Everything had seemed so real.

There's a perfectly logical explanation, I told myself firmly, walking closer to the bottom of the stairs so I could study the image. It wasn't exactly like in my dream after all: there were subtle differences. The window from last night had only featured the lady on the horse, but in real life, the picture was a whole scene, a painting spun so artfully in glass that it shimmered with life.

A young man with his head cast back in supplication knelt before the fierce, copper-haired lady in an emerald dress. Again, she rode the rearing blood-red horse. She didn't have a knife this time, though. Instead, she held a tightly bound scroll of paper in one hand, tied with a scarlet ribbon. Behind her was a large, shaggy black dog, looking over his shoulder at some riders on the horizon. Light streamed in through the window making the picture vividly alive. I could almost imagine the horse would leap out of the glass at any second.

"Admiring the Dark Lady, are you?" A thick, gravelly voice said right behind me.

I whirled around, yelping in surprise. The stooped elderly man I'd seen earlier in Xan's room stood by the front door. He looked much calmer now and his wild white hair had been combed carefully across his head in a wave. He wore a green, tweed jacket that hung about three sizes too big on his spare frame. His face was creased with a network of wrinkles as if he'd spent his whole life outdoors in rough weather. He leaned his weight on a thick, gnarled cane that had been polished to a high shine. Just like the one that had been used to bludgeon Great Aunt Ruth in my dream.

I stared at it with wide eyes until I had my breathing under control. *Come on, Jilly, pull yourself together.* Of course, it was just my overactive imagination playing up again. He was just some harmless old man my subconscious had used to play a part in my nightmare.

He stared at me suspiciously with narrowed eyes and I realized he was waiting for me to answer his question.

"P ... pardon?"

His gaze shifted upward to lump on my head where the bandage had been and he lowered his bushy eyebrows ominously. "I asked if you were admiring the Dark Lady. She's a museum piece, that one. People used to come on tours a few times a year just to study it and take photos of the glass. They wanted to see the rest of the house too, of course, but she was the main attraction."

"It's ... it's beautiful," I said, backing away a little under his hostile gaze. "Did you call her the Dark Lady? Like the name of the farm?"

"Yes," he said sharply, "the farm was named after an old local legend. It's a silly tale for gossiping women if you ask me. What are you doing out here creeping around by yourself anyway? Looking for something in particular?"

"I'm not creeping," I said, a little defensively. "I'm simply *looking* for the front door so I can go check on my horse. I don't think there's anything sneaky about that."

"Maybe. Maybe not," he said doubtfully. "The door's right there in plain sight, though. Come on, this way to the stable then, if that's where you're *really* going."

For such a hunched old man, he moved surprisingly fast and, after the last two exhausting days, I had to work to keep up with him. By the time we'd crossed the neglected lawn, then the gravel driveway and were halfway to the barn, I was puffing with exertion. I had to stop. I closed my eyes to catch my breath and when I opened them again, I paused to truly take in my surroundings.

"Wow," I whispered under my breath as I took in the scenery. The house had been built on a slight rise and miles of rolling, forested hills stretched out before me; burnt yellow, orange, and red by the passing of Autumn.

I turned to face the house. Even though it was unkempt at the moment, it was just as striking on the outside as it was inside. A huge, sprawling, white mansion topped with windowed peaks. Even in its run-down state, it was grander than Greystone. It must have been fantastic back in its day.

As I stared up at the house in appreciation, a movement in one of the second-floor windows caught my eye. Despite the crisp weather, one of the upper dormers had been left ajar and the bottom of a white curtain had blown outward and flapped lazily in the breeze.

A figure stood half-hidden by the billowing fabric. A pale face, an emerald dress and piercing blue eyes that bore into mine even from this distance.

I blinked and she was gone. The curtain was tucked inside and all the windows were shut tight.

I hope I'm not going crazy, I thought worriedly, frowning and touching the sore place on my head. Maybe hallucinations were a sign of a concussion.

"Come on, keep up," the old man grumbled from up ahead, and I hurried after him.

The front of the barn was a little tidier than the lawn but not by much. There was a path mowed up to the barn door but otherwise, the grass stood knee-high against the stable. It looked like it hadn't been tended in months.

"Here," the man said grumpily, throwing open the big double doors. "Come see them then since you're so anxious. You're just like Estelle and Ruth, always fussing over these horses."

I stepped inside, inhaling the rich smell of horse, leather, and hay that was so familiar and dear to me.

What a funny-looking place, I thought as soon as my eyes had adjusted to the light. The barn was a dramatic mixture of ancient and modern. The spot closest to us was obviously part of the original stables; the walls were made of thick, crumbling old stone and overhead were dark exposed beams. The stalls were stone, too, with heavy iron bars running vertically across the fronts. It looked dark and foreboding, more like a dungeon than a stable.

About a third of the way down, the atmosphere changed completely where the new addition had been added. The walls were wooden instead of stone and the arched ceiling overhead was made of honey-coloured wood.

I suppose they wanted to keep the history of the place alive, I thought, *but I sure like the modern part better. This section gives me the chills.*

The long concrete aisle that spanned both sections looked like it hadn't been swept in days, bits of hay and straw lay everywhere.

As I stepped inside, horses popped their heads over the doorways one by one, gazing at us curiously. It was a good sign; usually only well-treated horses were eager to meet new people. A whole barn full of happy horses made me feel a little more relaxed.

A familiar grey head stared at me hopefully from halfway down the aisle and my heart leapt when I saw him. I couldn't get to his side fast enough.

"Bally." I stepped inside his stall and wrapped my arms tightly around his elegant neck. "I was so worried about you."

He blew warm breath on my face and nuzzled my pockets gently, looking for treats. After a few minutes, he politely extracted himself from my hug and went back to his hay.

He looked the picture of health. He was bedded deeply in fresh straw and had a manger full of hay and a bucket of fresh water. Someone had put on his light, plaid stable blanket and he looked snug as a bug.

"You happy now?" the man said from right outside Bally's

stall, making me jump again. He had an awful way of creeping up without making a sound.

"Yes," I said honestly, "He looks wonderful. Was it you who took such good care of him?"

"Maybe it was," the man said gruffly, but he looked a little pleased.

After assuring myself that Bally was fine, I moved to check on Rigel and found him looking just as well-cared for, although he pinned his ears at me in a threatening way that clearly meant he did not want to be hugged. Ever.

"Thank you so much for taking care of them," I told the elderly man again. "We didn't mean to be a bother to you. We were invited to see Aunt Ruth, but then I suppose my cousin Xan mixed the dates up and we came at the wrong time. I'm Jilly, by the way," I said, holding out my hand to him, "and you are…..?"

He looked down at my hand in consternation and for a moment I thought he'd turn around and leave without answering. His mouth worked up and down a few times and finally, he grudgingly reached out and shook my hand with his rough, gnarled one.

"Jacob," he said reluctantly, clearing his throat a few times as if being polite was a colossal effort.

"Well, it's nice to meet you. How many horses do you have here?"

Again, there was that pause as if he were judging how much information to share with me.

"Twenty, right now," he said finally. "Sometimes there are more, sometimes less."

I followed him back down the aisle, admiring the well-bred horses as we passed.

"Oh, you have a young one," I exclaimed when we reached the section where the old stone began. I stood on my toes to look over the stall door. A shaggy dark colt lifted his head from the manger, trailing a mouthful of hay. He looked very tiny inside that massive stone cell.

"I always love foaling season at home. Sometimes I think I like the breeding program better than riding. What is he? What are his bloodlines?"

"No idea," Jacob answered in a surly voice. "I don't know anything about fancy-pants bloodlines and all that mumbo jumbo. I leave that to Ruthie and Estelle. I just know that he eats and makes a mess like the rest of them."

Ruthie? I thought in surprise. I'd never heard anyone call Great Aunt Ruth a nickname of any sort unless you counted the younger cousins christening her Great Aunt Ruthless. Old Jacob almost sounded as if he *liked* her. Perhaps he was a little senile.

"Well, I think he's lovely," I said, gazing at the young horse affectionately. He was in that awkward stage between baby and grown-up where all his parts were laughably out of proportion. His head was a little too big for his neck, his legs too long for his body, and his hind end a good two inches taller than his front end. If he were a human then he'd be a gawky fourteen-year-old boy. His fuzzy coat was dark brown, almost black, with just a thin streak of white between his wide, intelligent eyes.

"Would it be all right if I went in to see him?"

"I don't suppose it would hurt," Jacob said grudgingly. "I have to do some things in the feed room. I'll be around to keep half an eye on you to make sure you stay out of trouble."

I didn't bother to answer that. I slid back the bolt and pushed opened the heavy door, glad to see that the little horse stepped boldly toward me, not pushy, but curious and calm. I held out my hand and smiled as his little whiskers brushed across my fingers before nuzzling my arm and gently touching my cheek. His breath was warm and sweet, and his big eyes stared curiously into mine.

He reached down to sniff my pockets carefully and then,

realizing that I didn't have any treats, he turned back to his lunch. He didn't object when I offered to scratch the spot just near his shoulder blades that most horses like, or when I combed out his short, silky mane with my fingers.

"Your stall needs to be cleaned, little one," I said, frowning. Unlike Bally's stall, this one hadn't been picked out in days. It didn't smell very nice, either. The stone surrounding us looked damp and crumbling and like the whole thing needed a good scrub.

"All right," Jacob said gruffly, appearing again, "time to go. I have other things to do. I don't know what it is with you girls fawning all over horses. You spoil them."

His sharp words were softened when he sent me the barest of smiles. I had the feeling that, *very deep* behind his crusty exterior, Jacob was a bit of a softy. I followed him outside, wishing I could have stayed in the barn longer.

"How many barn workers do you have here, Jacob?" I asked as we shut the big front door behind us.

I was just trying to make polite conversation but my innocent question set him off again. He lowered his bushy eyebrows at me suspiciously and jerked his chin down like a bull lowering its horns and getting ready to charge.

"None of your beeswax," he said roughly, "come on, back to the house with you. I have better things to do than entertain nosy, meddling women all day."

"Oh, I'm sorry," I said in bewilderment. "I didn't mean to offend you."

He glared over his shoulder at me and then his face softened just a little.

"Well, maybe you didn't. Maybe you're harmless and maybe you're not. I can't tell just by looking at you."

"Why would you think I'm harmful?" I asked in astonishment, hurrying to catch up with him.

"No reason!" he snapped. "Stop asking me so many questions. You're getting me all muddled up. Estelle said that I wasn't to say anything to nobody."

"Okay," I said slowly, my mind working overtime to try and sort out everything he'd said. "Well, you certainly haven't told me anything private, Jacob. I don't think you'll get in trouble. I'm sorry to have upset you."

"Oh, it's not just you. Everything's been all topsy-turvey lately. I'm exhausted taking care of all those horses, and now that Estelle is injured, I'm going to have to look after them all myself. I'm too old for this, I tell you."

"You just have two people to take care of all those horses?" I asked gently. "Where are all the farmhands?"

"Gone," he said sharply. "She sent them all away because we didn't know who to trust. So now it's just me and Estelle who do all the work."

"Who sent them away, Jacob?" I asked patiently, but it was one question too many.

He stepped back, abruptly raising his cane defensively between us as if he were blocking himself from an attack. His face turned a florid shade of red, and he worked his mouth up and down a few times as if at a loss to find the right words to convey his ire.

"You mind your own business, Miss Troublemaker," he finally spit out. "You come here prying with all your fancy questions trying to get me to tell you things. Well, you'll get nothing from me. Nothing. You get back where you came from."

My jaw dropped and I stared at him in complete shock. What on earth had brought on this outburst? It wasn't like we'd tried to rob the place or anything. It wasn't our fault that Estelle was hurt, after all. We'd been the ones to rescue her.

But before I could say any of that, the colour drained from his face and he clutched at his chest. Dropping his cane he reached a gnarled hand toward me, his fingers digging into my sleeve, clutching my coat like a lifeline.

"Jacob." I reached out to steady him. "What's wrong? Are you ill?"

"Pills," he wheezed, "in the house."

"Come on," I said quickly, "hold onto my arm, I'll help you get into the house and we'll find your medication."

Together, we hobbled the rest of the way to the manor. I wrenched open the heavy front door and helped Jacob to sit on an antiquated, carved wooden bench just inside.

"Help," I called, my voice echoing loudly around the wide entry hall. "Someone help."

A door slammed deep inside the house, and then another one closer by. Aimee came running down the stairs, her blonde hair in disarray. She froze on the bottom step, looking at Jacob in horror. From a room nearby, Xan appeared, supporting a thin, dark-haired woman who I instantly recognized as the girl from the woods, Estelle. She had a livid bruise over one cheekbone, an air-cast on one leg, and dark circles under her eyes.

She's the girl from my dream last night, I thought in alarm, *I didn't recognize her until just now.*

I looked at her uneasily, remembering again the horrible role she'd played in my dream; it was hard to erase the image of her about to bludgeon my aunt to death.

Xan was clean-shaven and freshly dressed, and I could smell his cologne from halfway down the hall. He had an arm hovering behind the girl's back and there was a starry look in his eye that I'd never seen him wear before.

"Oh, Jacob," Estelle said, putting a hand over her mouth when she saw the state Jacob was in, "Aimee, don't just stand there. Run upstairs and get his pills. Quickly."

A look of what might have been irritation passed over Aimee's face.

"Yes, Estelle," she said tightly, "whatever you say." But then she glanced over at Jacob whose face had turned an ominous shade of grey and she quickly turned and ran up the stairs as fast as she could.

"Just breathe, Jacob, nice and easy like the doctor showed you," Estelle, said gently, leaning on Xan as she came to sit next to the old man. "Aimee will be back in a flash with your medication."

"I didn't say a word, Estelle," he wheezed, "I didn't tell her nothing. These city folk think they can just walk in here…"

He broke off in series of violent wheezing coughs that shook his whole body.

"Of course, you didn't," Estelle soothed, shooting an anxious glance at me, "you've done everything just right, just like Ruthie would want. You just rest now. Aimee should be back any second."

She looked up the staircase, frowning, probably wondering what was taking Aimee so long.

"Here they are," the young maid called as she rushed down the stairs. "I couldn't find them at first. Here, Jacob, take this."

He opened his mouth and she expertly popped both pills inside. "Sorry, I didn't have time to get water. Just get them down as best you can."

Jacob swallowed hard and then leaned his head back against the wall with his eyes closed. After a few minutes, the colour in his face returned and he started to look much better.

"Why don't you let Aimee take you upstairs so you can have a good rest?" Estelle said gently.

"All right, I'll go see Ruthie. She always makes me feel better."

There was an awkward pause.

"You know Ruth is away," Aimee said sharply, rolling her eyes. "You'll see her when she gets back from vacation, just like the rest of us."

"Of course, he knows that," Estelle said kindly, patting the old man's hand, "he just forgot. Go up to bed, Jacob. I'll be up to check on you soon."

She watched anxiously as Aimee led the old man, not overly gently, up the stairs.

"I'm so sorry about that," she said as soon as they were out of earshot. "He's a wonderful man and he's been with Ruth for years, but I'm afraid that his mind may be slipping. It's the stress."

"What sort of stress?" I asked, curious.

"Oh, well," she flushed and looked down at the floor. "It's not my place to say. Ruth has her reasons for the things she does and it's not up to me to question them." She paused and bit her lip. "It's just, well, she sent away most of the house and stable help two months ago and it left everyone a little overwhelmed with all the chores to do. It wasn't so bad in the summer when the horses were mostly turned out on grass but now, with winter coming, I'm not sure what we'll do. It's a big estate and I'm afraid we can't keep up with it. It's getting run-down and the repairs that need to be done keep piling up. Jacob has been here all his life and I know it upsets him to see things so untidy, but he's too old to take care of it himself."

"But why would she do that?" I asked in astonishment. I knew firsthand how many people it took to run a massive estate. We had dozens of housekeepers, gardeners, and stable-help to make Greystone run like clockwork; it practically took an army.

Estelle took a deep breath. "I really can't say. I'm sorry, but Ruth is my boss and my friend, and I can't talk about her behind her back. I expect she'll fill you in on everything when she ... er, gets back from vacation."

"But then, this is perfect timing," Xan said excitedly. "Its fate, really; we came exactly when you needed us. We'll just stay on and help you until Aunt Ruth gets back."

"Oh, no, no, no." Estelle drew away from him, all the

colour fading from her already pale cheeks. "That will not be necessary *at all*. Thank you but you must go home tomorrow, as planned."

"Nonsense," Xan said, oblivious to the look of rising panic on her face. "We'd planned to be away for two weeks. That will give us enough time to spruce the place up. Jilly and I can help with the horses and our manservant can help Jacob with all the mowing and landscaping."

I choked at the word *manservant* and looked around quickly to make sure Gilbert was nowhere in earshot.

"Absolutely not," Estelle said, "I can't let you do it. In fact, I forbid it. Ruthie would hate …"

"… to have imposed on us. I know, but that's what family does for one another. We help out when times are tough. Don't we, Jilly?"

"Er, yes," I said uncertainly, watching Estelle with concern. Her face had gone several shades of pale in succession and now a fine sheen of sweat glistened on her forehead.

"Xan, I think you'd better get Estelle a glass of water, she looks—"

But it was too late, she toppled over in front of us and Xan caught her just before she hit the floor.

Chapter 5

*A*fter that, it was impossible to change Xan's mind about staying. Despite reasoning, pleading and threats, nothing Estelle, Aimee, or Jacob said could budge him from his new purpose. And when Xan set his mind to something there was no point in arguing.

"You need us," was all he'd say, "and we're not leaving until this place is spruced up. You can tell Aunt Ruth to blame me when she gets back."

Finally, grudgingly, they didn't have much choice but to give in.

"One week," Estelle said firmly, "that's all you have. And then you have to promise to go back to where you came from."

"It's a deal," Xan said happily, although knowing him he probably had his fingers and toes crossed. The way he was hovering protectively over Estelle with that starry-eyed expression made me think that he never planned to leave.

Even though I didn't feel comfortable staying somewhere where I wasn't exactly wanted, I was determined to help out as much as I could. Gilbert, however, did not feel quite so gracious about it.

"He called me a manservant, Jilly."

"I know he did, Gil. And I apologize for him. He sometimes says stupid things without thinking. But couldn't you find it in your heart to help Jacob? Just for a few days. It would make him so happy to see the place cleaned up."

Gil had stomped away without answering, but later I saw him lugging the ancient push-mower out to the front lawn with Jacob hobbling along beside him giving loud, imperious directions.

Poor Gil, I thought guiltily, *I always get him caught up in these messes.*

But since he was occupied, my first order of business was to get that barn clean.

"I suppose I'd better come and show you where everything is," Estelle had said, still looking irritated. She hadn't completely resigned herself to the fact that we were staying and she shot Xan a sharp glance when he reached out to steady her.

Aimee had dug up an old pair of crutches for her somewhere, and she limped slowly beside us across the lawn, Xan hovering about an inch away with his hand out, ready to catch her if she so much as stumbled.

"It was awful timing for me to get hurt," Estelle said, blushing a little when we reached the barn, "it's probably a bit of a mess in there."

"Accidents happen,' I reassured her. "Why don't we start by turning everyone out on pasture and then we can start cleaning?" I was itching to get those stalls spotless; horses to me were a gift and should never have to stand around in dirty stalls.

We rolled open the big front barn doors and I smiled automatically as I stepped inside. There was something about facing a barn full of horses that made my heart go pitter-patter. I went to see Bally first and scratched his neck affectionately.

"Which horses are yours to ride?" I asked Estelle when she limped up to Bally's stall door.

"Well, right now I guess I'm responsible for all of them. We had two more riders before Ruthie let them go, and in the summer, we had extra grooms who could warm them up and cool them out for me between rides. But, for the last couple of months it's been just Jacob, Ruthie, and me trying to keep up."

There's that nickname again, I thought. *Ruth must be a much kinder person at home than she ever was visiting Greystone.*

"We sold quite a few of the young stock already so we're down to only twenty horses. Many of those are broodmares, though, and they don't get ridden. I pretty much decided to lay off most of the show horses for the winter and only keep five or six of the best sales horses in work. That's all I can handle. Or could handle before now, I guess," Estelle added, looking down sadly at her air-cast.

She showed me the chart on the wall that listed which pastures everyone went in, and one by one Xan and I led them out. They were mostly well-mannered and pleasant and didn't give much trouble. Even Rigel behaved himself, although I noticed that Xan didn't let his guard down for a single second while he was leading him.

"Oh, I've met this guy already," I said, looking in at my fuzzy little yearling friend from the morning. "What is his name?"

"His registered name is DL Damascus. We haven't gotten around to giving him a barn name yet, but Jacob calls him The Ugly Duckling. He's a bit of a disappointment, actually; he's from our own breeding program and we had high hopes for him, but he's turned out quite plain and undersized. Ruth was too embarrassed to send him to the sale with the other young stock; we would have been laughed out of the building."

"Oh, but he's just a baby," I protested, "lots of them take a long time to mature; I bet he'll turn out to be nice."

"Don't mind her," Xan said jokingly, coming up behind us, "Jilly always has a thing for the underdogs. She likes taking care of mangy strays."

I shot him a dark look, knowing that he was including Gil in that statement.

"I guess there's always a chance he'll surprise us," Estelle said dryly, "watch him, though, he's liable to trip and fall on you."

It turned out that Damascus *was* a bit of a mess; his long legs weren't very coordinated and he stumbled into me every few seconds. He swung his head around to look at everything, eyes wide as if he hadn't left his stall in months, although Estelle had said they'd all been out two days ago. He tried to prance beside me but ended up stumbling over his own feet. He pretended to nip and then hung his head with his ears drooping gloomily to the side when I gently reprimanded him. He was indeed a sensitive soul.

I turned him out with some of the older broodmares and watched him carefully as he skipped away to join them.

I bet I'm right, I thought as he cantered clumsily toward them, *someday he's going to grow into those legs and turn into a fantastic horse.*

"I'm sorry," Estelle said when I got back, "but that's all we have for pasture. I don't have room for your horse to go out."

"Would you mind if I just let him loose around the yard?" I asked hopefully, "he's very well-behaved. He'll just eat and not cause any trouble."

"I guess so," she said, looking surprised, "as long as you're sure he won't injure himself. He looks expensive."

"He won't get hurt. Bally is the most sensible horse I've ever met."

Just then, impatient at being left until last, Bally reached his nose out of his stall and gently slid back the bolt to his door, letting himself politely into the aisle.

"Oh goodness, he's loose," Estelle said in alarm, sounding like it was a tiger prowling toward her rather than kind, gentle Bally.

"He does it all the time at home." I laughed and gently tugged on his mane, encouraging him to follow me down the aisle into the sunshine outside. "I'm just surprised he waited this long to let himself out."

True to form, as soon as he saw grass Bally dropped his head and immediately began grazing when I parked him in the middle of a lush patch in front of the barn. I was sure he could happily spend the whole day there eating.

"Wow, I would never trust any of my horses to do that," Estelle said, looking at Bally enviously. "They'd take off for the hills and never come back."

"You never know, they might surprise you," I said quietly. It always saddened me when people who loved horses only thought of the riding and grooming and missed out on building a trusting, playful friendship. In my eyes, that was the very best part of being around horses.

"Oh, don't mind her," Xan said with a laugh. "I wouldn't trust my horses loose either. Jilly can get any horse to follow her around like a dog. That's what happens when you spend all your time in the barn and have no social life at all," Xan teased.

I stuck my tongue out at him playfully and shrugged. He'd hit the nail on the head there.

"You should have seen her with my old horse, Teddy. I think he would have done anything to please her. She even taught him to bow on command. That didn't impress the judge very much at the end of our dressage test, I can tell you."

We all laughed again, but I felt another pang when I remembered what a sweet, trusting horse Teddy had been. I hoped he'd found a good, permanent home with someone who loved and appreciated him more than Xan had.

Finally, with all the horses out we were able to get to work cleaning stalls.

"I'm so sorry, Jill," Estelle said wearily as I came back pushing my second wheelbarrow load. "I'm going to have to go lie down. This has been a little much for me."

"I'll escort you back," Xan said quickly, gathering her crutches. "You'll be okay here by yourself, Jilly?"

"Um ..." I looked down the long line of dirty stalls dubiously, "I suppose ..."

"Great," he said, tossing his pitchfork aside, "we'll see you at lunch."

Sighing heavily at his typical Xan behaviour, I resigned myself to a full day of heavy labour. Technically, I wasn't supposed to clean our stalls at home, since there were paid employees to do the grunt work, but I helped out anyway whenever Mother was otherwise occupied. So, I knew what I was doing.

Still, this wasn't like cleaning our impeccable stable at home where every stall was picked out three or four times a day. Besides Bally and Rigel's stalls, the rest of them hadn't been cleaned in days. The straw bedding was heavy and wet; the sharp smell of ammonia made my eyes water.

By the time I was a quarter of the way through, my arms ached, sweat beaded my forehead, and there was an unidentified green smear across one cheek.

"Do you need a hand?"

"Gil," I said, looking up with undisguised relief. "I'd love some help, thank you. This stuff is heavy."

We worked in companionable silence for a few minutes.

"Jilly, something's been bothering me about the other night."

I looked up at him in surprise. Surely, he wasn't embarrassed about falling asleep in my room. If anything, he should be ashamed of all the snoring he'd done.

"How did you fall off Bally?"

"Oh," I said, startled. I hadn't expected that at all. "I don't know. That night is all mixed up in my head; I still can't sort out what's a dream and what isn't."

Gilbert leaned on his pitchfork and waited patiently for me to go on.

"I mean, what I do remember doesn't make any sense."

"Why don't you tell me what you think happened from beginning to end and don't worry if it doesn't make sense. We can piece it together later."

"Well," I hesitated, "I remember us driving with the horse trailer; I know we came here with Xan to see Great Aunt Ruth. Then there's a big gap until Bally and I found Xan and Estelle in the woods. I remember galloping to find help for Estelle and arriving at that fork in the road. This is where it gets really strange. This angry lady in an old-fashioned dress appeared out of nowhere on a horse. She said a lot of bizarre things and then pointed out the right road to me. Obviously, that part had to be a dream. Then I think I remember galloping up to the house. I thought I stopped just in front of the lawn, but then after that, it's all muddled. There were people there and ... and I think I remember lying in the front hallway. That's it until I woke up in bed."

"Bally had his reins draped over a branch, Jilly. Your helmet was sitting on a bench nearby," he said solemnly, "and his stirrups had been run up."

"Oh?" I said in surprise. "Well, I suppose someone found us there and took care of him. A horse person would have probably run his stirrups up and set my helmet somewhere safe so he didn't step on it."

"What horse person? Estelle was hurt and I can't see any of the others doing it."

"Xan? Maybe he saw Bally on his way in?"

"No, I asked him. There wasn't a mark on your helmet,

either." Gil stabbed his pitchfork into the dirty straw. "Not even dust. There's a lump on your head the size of an orange. If your helmet had been on when you got that injury, it would have been crushed or dented. It was pristine."

"Okay," I said slowly, "so, what are you saying? I took my helmet off for some reason and then I fell off? Maybe I was on the ground and Bally spooked and knocked me over."

"Maybe," he said grimly. "Or maybe something else happened."

"What are you thinking?"

"I'm not sure, Jilly. I just think we should be on guard just in case. There's something funny going on here."

I thought about that drugged glass of orange and suppressed a little shiver. What if it hadn't been an accident at all? The staff had made no secret that they'd wanted us to leave. And yet I couldn't see any of them trying to hurt us on purpose. Aimee had seemed genuinely distressed about the orange juice incident.

I mulled it all over in brooding silence while we worked. With two people cleaning, the work went quickly and soon the stable was spic and span again. The stalls were deeply bedded in clean, fluffy straw, the water buckets were scrubbed and filled, and each manger topped with fragrant, green hay.

By the time we were done sweeping the aisle, my stomach was rumbling loudly for lunch.

"I don't think I want to put a helmet on yet, Gil, my head's still too sore," I admitted. "Do you think you could ride Bally for me today? I don't want him having too many days off and it gives us an excuse to check out the fancy indoor arena."

Gil shot me a sideways look. "You don't want Xan to ride him?"

"Oh no," I said quickly. "Bally wouldn't like that at all. Besides, he's used to you. Please?"

"Well, when you ask so nicely, how can a guy resist?"

"Exactly," I said, elbowing him gently in the ribs. "You are putty in my hands."

Gil's smile dropped away and he sighed heavily. "Sometimes, that's what I worry about."

We stopped outside the barn to check on Bally and found him still knee-deep in grass, happily doing his part to keep the lawn mowed.

I went over and hugged him, then leaned against his broad, warm shoulder and happily gazed around. Even though, as vacations went, this one was a bit of a disaster, it was still so nice to be away from home. I swear the further I got from Greystone and my mother, the better I felt.

I closed my eyes for a second, basking in the afternoon sunshine, and when I opened them, I found Gil watching me with a smile on his face.

"What?" I asked, smiling back at him automatically. Right then he looked like the carefree old Gil of my childhood.

"It's just nice to see you happy and relaxed again. You remind me of the girl I used to know."

"Funny, I was just thinking the same thing about you. You don't let your guard down very often either, my friend."

He sighed and rubbed a hand across his face. "I know. I'm sorry. This whole thing has just been so hard, you know."

"What thing?" I asked in confusion. "Coming to Dark Lady Farms?"

"No, not that," he said impatiently, "You. The fact that you changed overnight and you still haven't come back to me. I keep waiting for you to come back. I know you don't like to talk about it, Jilly, but after that day we nearly drowned, the day Nanny was fired, that was the beginning of a nightmare for me. I wasn't allowed to see you for months, and then you got sick and were whisked away to Europe.

When you came home it was like you'd become an entirely different person."

I stared at him in astonishment. We never spoke about our near-drowning or what happened afterward. It was much too painful, even after all this time. It made me physically sick to talk about it, even now.

"I didn't change, Gil," I said slowly. "I mean, I was upset about Nanny of course, but I was still me. I'm still the same person."

"Were you? Are you?" he asked bluntly, looking deep into my eyes.

"Well, I …" I swallowed hard. It was true that I'd never felt quite myself again after that summer. I guess I'd put a big piece of myself away with the rest of my childhood things, like the silly ghosts I'd made up. But that was just a part of growing up, wasn't it? My stomach lurched a little and I put a hand over my mouth. This was the way it always was when I talked about something difficult. My body just couldn't handle it. It's why I avoided conflict like the plague.

"Jilly, before you left you were brilliant. You were curious about the whole world and how it worked. You were a budding scientist, a writer, and an inventor; you were my funny, quirky genius friend. You could have done anything.

But then you came back and you were like a shell of your old self. You were polite and did what you were told. I can always feel the old you in there Jilly, simmering beneath the surface. But she never quite breaks free. You lost interest in everything but horses after that summer. I think the single thing you were interested in after that was Bally."

"Hey, that's not true," I said, feeling a little offended. I was still interested in things other than horses. I liked lots of things like … well, food, and walking out on the hills with Bally, and brushing Bally and riding him, and planning his training schedule, and planning for shows. Hmm, maybe Gil had a slight point.

"Do you remember you had those stacks of notebooks," Gil said suddenly, surprising me. "You wrote your ghost stories and your experiments and your hypotheses, and all sorts of things in them non-stop. You had so many dreams for the future. You shared them with me almost every night. And then it just ended."

"It did?" I asked uncertainly, trying to remember. That time of my life always felt foggy to me when I tried to recall it in detail.

"What did you did do with them?"

"The notebooks? I have no idea. I switched bedrooms when I came home from Europe. Mother must have tossed them out or packed them up somewhere. I haven't thought of them in years."

"They were important to you," Gil said stubbornly, "and you just threw them away like everything else."

I didn't like the way he was looking at me at all; like I'd betrayed him somehow.

"I ... I need to go inside now, my head hurts," I lied. Cold fear was bubbling up inside of me, alongside the nausea. I crossed my arms over my chest to keep my hands from shaking.

"And that's what you always do; change the subject when things get serious or uncomfortable. Ever since that summer you've avoided any sort of meaningful conversation."

"I don't know what you're talking about," I said, although I knew exactly what he meant. "I don't see why we just can't talk about pleasant things and get along."

Gil clenched his jaw and stalked away, leaving me trailing in his wake.

"Look, Gil," I said reasonably. "I'm happy enough like I am. I don't need to be anyone different. Don't you remember how often I used to get pushed over and teased when I was a kid? I don't need that sort of attention back in my life again. I don't need to be brilliant."

He turned on me in a flash, his face contorted with anger and pain and, surprisingly, fear.

I stepped back, almost crying out at the raw anguish on his face. I had never seen him look like that before. Not since…

"Whatever makes you happy, Jilly," he said, his dull voice not matching his expression at all. And then he turned and left me at the front door, striding off toward the woods.

I stared sadly at his retreating back, tears clouding my eyes. Why on earth did we fight about the silliest things? He was the last person I wanted to argue with; life was so good when we were getting along. And what had all that silly talk about my notebooks been? Why did he care so much about a tiny detail of our past?

My gaze drifted to a dark clump of bracken in the nearby woods and froze. A man was staring at me from the trees; he was too far away for me to make out his features but there was no mistaking the hostile, predatory way he stood. He took a step in my direction and every instinct in my body cried out for me to run. I felt like a field mouse watched by a hawk.

A deep, mournful howl rose from the woods nearby. The man flinched and disappeared like a flash into the forest. The bracken nearby crackled and a great, massive black dog shot out of the woods, gave me a glance from a pair of baleful, yellow eyes and then plunged back into the forest where the man had been.

For a moment I couldn't move, couldn't do anything but stare, but then I pulled myself together, yanked the door open and bolted inside, slamming it hard behind me.

Chapter 6

I stood with my back pressed firmly against the door, waiting for my wildly beating heart to find its rhythm again. What on earth had I just seen?

Something thumped on the landing and I glanced up only to hold back my second scream of the morning. Those baleful yellow eyes again but this time crafted from intricate bits of colour. That gargantuan dog poised at the foot of the Dark Lady's horse staring intently at me out of the glass. His eyes bored straight into mine almost as if he were trying to tell me something.

I gave a half-hysterical laugh and took a deep breath.

You are being ridiculous, I told myself firmly, *getting spooked by nothing. There probably wasn't even anything in the woods outside; just your imagination playing up again.*

I marched down the long hall toward my room, intent on changing out of my dirty barn clothes, having a good lunch, and putting the whole bizarre situation behind me when a nagging thought stopped me in my tracks.

Slowly, reluctantly I retraced my steps to the foot of the stairs and gazed upward, already guessing what I'd find.

The dog is facing the wrong way, I thought in dismay, *he's looking over his shoulder at the riders in the distance, just like he was when I first saw the stained glass. He was never looking my way at all. I am going crazy.*

Fear rippled through me. What if the blow to my head had made my harmless hallucinations worse? What if I stayed this way forever, never being sure of what was real and what wasn't? I'd spent my whole childhood living in a fantasy world; I would do anything to keep from going back that way again.

A dim memory surfaced, unbidden, of my fourteen-year-old self sobbing while my mother flew into one of her famous rages. "Do you want everyone laughing at you forever, Jillian? Don't you want to finally be friends with the other children? You have to put these silly things behind you."

I shook my head to clear it and walked the rest of the way to my room, wrapped in worry. I had no idea why all these memories were surfacing now. I thought I'd locked them all safely away.

I dug through my luggage until I found some clean clothes and heard a little clinking sound as I zipped my suitcase shut.

I looked down at the dresser to see that I'd knocked one of the little horse figurines over.

"Sorry, little one," I said, putting it upright again. I frowned, looking down at the group of sculptures more closely. I hadn't paid attention to them before but now I realized that they were all little replicas of the rider in the painting on my wall and in the stained-glass window. A lady in an emerald dress on a red horse. They weren't particularly well done, just cheap porcelain figures posed in a variety of ways; sometimes the horse was rearing or standing or running, and the lady alternated between having her arm upraised or sitting quietly, staring moodily off toward the horizon.

Great, I guess there's no escaping her anywhere, I thought, shaking my head. *Who would have so many versions of the same sculpture in one place?*

My first shower that morning had exhausted the hot water supply but I did my best with the tepid trickle while the copper pipes groaned and creaked in chorus.

When I came out of the bathroom, my bedroom door was open and Morris was sitting propped upright in the middle of my bed, his legs stuck out in opposite directions like turkey drumsticks while he did some personal grooming.

"Hello, silly cat," I said to him, scratching the top of his head a few times before leaving him to it. "I wonder what you've been eating these last three days. I can't see them having a supply of cat food here for you, and yet you look fat and happy. Probably dining on caviar and cream, aren't you?"

I loosely wove my hair into a long braid and pulled on my usual uniform of breeches and a long-sleeved shirt even though I wouldn't be riding today. They were still the most comfortable clothes I owned.

I padded out into the hall, my stomach rumbling. There was a light thump behind me and I turned to see Morris trotting after me, his orange, striped tail stuck straight up in the air like an exclamation mark.

"I wonder what's behind all these doors, Morris," I wondered aloud, and on impulse, I reached out and tried a handle. It turned easily and I peeked inside to see a guest room almost identical to my own, only this one was furnished in mossy green rather than red. The dresser nearest the door had a set of little horse figurines just like mine did.

Weird, I thought, stepping closer to look at the tiny statues. *Why would she have so many copies of the same statue?*

I picked up one of the figures and turned it over carefully, it was much nicer than the ones in my room had been. It was made of the most fragile porcelain, feeling almost hollow in my hands. It had been made with exquisite detail, even down to the expression of anger on the horse's face. There was a tiny makers-mark stamped on the bottom but I didn't recognize it. Mother had a lot of antiques and had dragged me all over the countryside in my youth in an effort to educate me, but I had been a poor student and had spent every moment wishing to be back at the barn.

I put that one down and picked up the next, this one was bigger and heavier and more clumsily made. It had a thickly painted set of initials at the bottom and a number that meant it was from a small batch of ten. Perhaps locally made.

I set the figurines back in exactly the same places and backed carefully out of the room. Now my curiosity was stirred a little and I peeked into a few more doors and found them nearly identical. All the guest rooms were decorated in their own colours; but the layouts were the same, right down to the little figurines on the dresser. By the fifth door I opened, it was starting to feel a little weird; either Great Aunt Ruth had zero imagination in decorating or she was strangely obsessed with this specific layout for some reason.

Finally, as I neared the end of the hall, I came to a room that was different than the rest. It was a small sitting room with plump leather chairs arranged in a comfortable way around a crackling fire. I wrinkled my nose as I stepped inside. The fire must have just been recently lit because the air was tinged with the acrid smell of burning.

A book sat splayed open and face down on a small table near the fire, the spine bent at an angle that made my book-loving self wince. Next to it was a half-full cup of tea, still faintly steaming.

"Hello?" I said tentatively, stepping into the room. A log popped in the fireplace, making me jump. "Is anyone here?"

There was no answer. I was about to leave when the fire crackled loudly again and a chunk of ash and paper shot onto the empty hearth and rolled across the short stretch to where the stone met the hardwood floor. We had many fireplaces at home and I knew how quickly an escaped ember could burn holes in the carpet or wood floors so I didn't hesitate to move toward it and grab the little metal dustpan that hung beside the hearth.

I shifted the burning debris onto the shovel and was about to throw it back into the flames when something about the smoldering paper caught my eye. It wasn't newspaper like you'd use to start a fire, this paper was thick and I could still see remnants of elegant, scrolled writing on one of the larger pieces. *Sound mind. Horses. Everything.* There were more words but the paper was too badly burned for me to make out what they said.

It's none of your business, I told myself firmly. *Stop snooping*. I dumped the whole pile back into the fireplace and stood up, brushing my hands together briskly.

I left the room, shutting the door tightly behind me and made my way quickly down the hallway, not brave enough to try any of the other doors.

When I reached the front entryway where the stained-glass window stood, I refused to look at it, marching resolutely past and down the opposite hallway where the faint tantalizing smell of food was coming from.

Finally, my nose led me to a wide-open door on the left. I peered into a spotlessly clean kitchen that was almost a replica of our kitchen back at Greystone. There was the same long wooden table and cheery yellow walls. Only the appliances were stainless steel instead of our white ones at home.

There was a clatter somewhere inside, and I stepped through the doorway tentatively, not sure of my welcome.

A plump figure bustled out of the walk-in pantry, carrying a tray loaded with baking supplies.

"Oh," I said, putting a hand over my mouth. Because the woman was an identical copy of our cook Betty back home, right down to the no-nonsense expression and the silvery hair pulled back into a loose bun.

The woman jerked in surprise when saw me, set the tray down hard on the wooden table and put a hand over her heart. "My word, you frightened me. Well, you must be one of those relatives who travelled out here from the big city. Aimee told me about you."

I was too surprised by her appearance to tell her that we only lived a day away and Maplegrove wasn't exactly a bustling metropolis. Although I supposed it wasn't nearly so isolated as her part of the world; we had cell service, for instance. I sat down in the chair she pulled out for me and smiled at her shyly, not able to believe that I wasn't talking to Betty.

"You look famished," she said, her expression transforming from stern to warm and grandmotherly all at once. She moved over to the stove and used an oven mitt to lift the lid off a big cast-iron pot. "I have some chili about ready to go if you wanted to try some."

"Oh yes, please," I said, sniffing the rich, spicy aroma appreciatively.

"And I have a loaf of crusty bread leftover from yesterday. You'll have a nice, big piece of that on the side. Will you eat here or in the breakfast room?"

"Here, please," I said eagerly and sat there as she set out my cutlery and napkin, and then placed my food down in front of me with a flourish.

I took a bite and closed my eyes in bliss. She was even more talented than Betty if it were possible.

I didn't say a word the whole time I was eating, but after I'd finished and she'd whisked my plate and bowl away, I risked saying out loud what I'd been thinking the whole time.

"I'm Jillian," I said, smiling shyly up at her, "and you must be Betty's sister Belinda. I remember her talking about you, but I didn't know you worked here."

The Curse of The Golden Touch

"Oh, of course," she said, beaming down at me. "You're little Jilly, then. I've heard all about you, too. Betty is quite fond of you, my dear; she always includes a note about what you're up to in her letters. We only see each other once or twice a year so we make sure to keep in touch through the mail. There are four of us working for your family, you know. Our other sister Edwina works at the Willowdale estate, and of course, our brother Jacob lives, er, works here, too."

"Oh," I said in astonishment. "Jacob is Betty's brother?"

"He certainly is, and mine, too. We've all been with your family since we were quite young ourselves. Our grandparents worked for your great-grandfather when he was in France, and I suppose we sort of inherited our positions once our parents retired."

"Hmm," I said, not sure how I felt about this information. There was something amazing and sort of, well, *reassuring* about whole generations of trustworthy people toiling away selflessly for our family. But something was disturbing about it, too. Betty was a brilliant cook and, by the little I'd tasted, her sister was probably just as good if not better; maybe they could have been world-class chefs with their own restaurants or cooking shows on television or something. Surely there was more to aspire to than working for *us*.

I glanced upward and noticed that the glass pantry door had a picture etched into it. It was a familiar-looking silhouette of a lady on a rearing horse. The theme was honestly getting a bit tiring.

"Belinda, what's with all the statues and paintings of the lady on the horse everywhere? Jacob said there was a legend that went with them."

"Oh, yes, but it's not just a legend; it's fact. The lady was a real person and I'm surprised you haven't heard of her yet, with her being a relative and all."

"What?" I asked in astonishment. "She was related to us?"

"Oh yes, way back. She's your Great Aunt Ruth's ancestor so she must be yours as well. She and her family were the original owners of Dark Lady Farm, although it had a different name at the time, of course. She was born here and this, sadly enough, is where she met her tragic demise."

"That's awful."

"Well, yes and no; she died for love and sometimes that makes things all right. I was just about to make an apple pie, but I could tell you the story while I work. Would you like that?"

"Oh yes, please." I always loved a good story. And pie.

Belinda bustled around, setting ingredients out on the big table to get the crust made first.

"Can I peel and cut these for you?" I asked tentatively, pointing at the big bowl of freshly-washed apples. Betty had sometimes let me help her in the kitchen when Mother was safely off the property.

"Well, you certainly don't have to. But I make a policy of never saying no to free labour."

She set the apples in front of me, along with a paring knife and bowls for the peels and cut apples. When I was settled, she began her story.

"The Lady's real name was Evangeline, just like the Acadian heroine in the poem by Longfellow. You know the one?"

I nodded thoughtfully, I'd spend many nights reading alone in our library back home and I had a special spot in my heart for poetry.

"Well, *this* Evangeline was the only daughter of a very wealthy but hard-hearted merchant named Lord Ascot who had no trace of goodness in his heart. Lady Ascot, Evangeline's mother, was a sweet lady who quickly withered, fell ill, and died under the tyranny of her husband, leaving her only daughter behind. Evangeline was known throughout the area for her

The Curse of The Golden Touch

kindness toward both people and animals. She had a tender heart and couldn't pass a person in need without giving them a kind word or some money; a trait which enraged her miserly father.

"Evangeline used to roam the countryside on her horse, a huge, red bad-tempered beast that only she was able to handle and a massive black dog. She tirelessly brought fresh baked goods and donations to local orphanages and churches; going anywhere she was needed. She never needed a chaperone; everyone who knew her loved her, and both horse and dog would have guarded her with their lives.

"When she was just seventeen years old, Evangeline stopped in at the church and found a young man being cared for there, injured and feverish from his wounds. He had been a fur trapper for her father's company, but when he'd caught his leg in a trap and had just barely managed to creep into town, her father had refused to help him and had thrown him out onto the street. The church took him in but they were overburdened with a local influenza outbreak and could not pay for the doctor or care for him as much as he needed. The young man, Phillipe, was near to dying from his untreated wounds.

"Evangeline was outraged at her father's treatment of the young man and rode for the doctor as fast as she could. She paid for the visit and the medicines out of her own pocket and stayed by the young man's bedside as long as she dared. Every day she came to take care of him. Gradually, under her tender care, he recovered and the two young people found that they shared many things in common. Evangeline brought books to read to him and he'd sit very quietly, enraptured by her stories. When she tired, he would tell her tales of his life as a trapper and how much he missed his cabin in the woods.

"Evangeline loved to hear him tell of his cabin, she could picture every last detail of it. How the maple trees crowded round it, and how snug and cheerful it looked at night, lit up against the backdrop of snow.

"At home in her cold, palatial house, Evangeline would close her eyes and imagine that they lived in that cozy cabin, just the two of them, far away; where her father could never yell at her again. It was impossible, she knew; Phillipe was too poor and her father would never allow her to marry a lowly trapper, but still, she held her dream close to her heart.

"Phillipe, of course, felt the same but he knew he could never ask for her hand.

"The months passed, slowly he healed and soon, his time there would be over and he would have to go back to the woods.

"One evening, the week before he was to return, he was surprised to hear the sound of galloping hooves riding up to the little cottage he'd been staying in behind the church. It was nearly dark and he'd said goodbye to Evangeline hours ago, so he was shocked when she came flying up the path on foot and leapt into his arms, sobbing as if her heart would break.

"Phillipe had never allowed himself to touch Evangeline in anything else but brotherly formality, but he couldn't stop himself from wrapping his arms around her and gathering her shaking body protectively to his chest.

"Are you hurt," he asked, "Has anyone hurt you?"

"He could barely understand her tearful response but he finally heard the word "engaged" and his heart sank. He drew her carefully to a little bench and took off his thick travelling cloak to wrap around her shivering shoulders. She was dressed in a fancy, emerald evening dress, her tousled hair had been damaged by her wild ride but he could see that it had been held in place with diamond clips, any one of which could pay his salary for a year.

"He has auctioned me off to one of his greedy old friends just as if I were a horse in the market." Evangeline sobbed. "I will have to marry that horrible man and go live in his horrible house and be his wife. I would rather die than marry him."

"Hush, hush." Phillipe pressed her tightly to his chest and ran his fingers through her tousled hair.

"Evangeline, it's late, you have to get home now or people will talk. Everything will look brighter in the morning. We'll figure it out together."

"Reluctantly, Evangeline rose to her feet.

"What they didn't know was that the alarm had already been raised at home; at that moment, Lord Ascot, fueled into a wild frenzy by alcohol, had formed his guests into a search party and was right then bearing down upon the little church cottage.

"A house servant had already tearfully confessed that Evangeline had been seen by the church with Phillipe many times and now her outraged father was out for blood. Just then, there was a thunder of hooves and shouting voices coming from the woods. "There's a light by the church!" someone cried, "It must be her."

"No!" Evangeline recognized her father's grey stallion and she tore from Phillipe and ran toward her waiting horse. "I won't go back with them."

"Evangeline, wait, be reasonable," Phillipe begged, hobbling after her. But he was too late. She'd already leapt on her horse and wheeled it around.

"Hurry," she'd cried urgently. "We can still get away. We can hide in your cabin away from everyone. They won't find me there. We can have the life we always dreamed of."

"We can't run away," Phillipe said, "we have to be practical. If we can just sit down and talk ..."

"Talk," she spat. "Phillipe, you don't understand. They're going to kill you. Run away from here and go to your cabin in the woods; live a good life for me. Be happy."

"And with that, she clapped her heels to her horse's sides

and sped off into the darkness, the black dog following her like a shadow.

"She stopped to look back from the top of the nearby hill just in time to see the party of hunters swerve away from the church and charge up the hillside after her. Sure that she'd given Phillipe time to get away, she galloped hard in the opposite direction, urging her horse on hard.

"There was a sound of gunshots and a yelp of pain and she turned around just in time to see her great, beautiful dog felled to the ground in cold blood.

"With a wail of rage, she plunged into the forest. It was a dark night and she was too distraught to heed where she was going and rode blindly toward the cliffs that lined the township. Her horse faltered at the edge of the precipice but, not realizing the danger, she drove him on and the two of them leapt over the edge into the darkness below. The spot where she perished is right at the back of this property, but the cliff itself runs all the way close to town and ends in what the locals call Dark Lady Falls. That's what the farm's named after."

"That is so sad," I said, struck to the core by the tragic story.

"It was a terrible thing. The entire village went into mourning when Evangeline died. Her father declined rapidly, aging almost overnight. Shunned by the villagers, his business floundered and finally died. He was forced to flee the country to escape creditors and he was never heard from again. The estate lay empty for over ten years before a cousin came to take it over.

"The locals are very attached to the legend. They say that Evangeline's ghost wanders the woods between here and the village, still looking for her lost love. They say she sometimes appears to help those who have lost their way or to help star-crossed lovers find happiness."

I shivered despite the warmth of the kitchen, feeling inexplicably sad. sad.

"At least she had a taste of love and she followed her heart," Belinda said, reaching out to pat my arm. "That's something that many people never allow themselves to do. Even some folks here right under this very roof, I could mention."

"But, wait, what happened to Phillippe?"

"Nobody knows. He was never seen again so it was supposed that he went back to his cabin in the woods and lived out his life."

"Oh, honestly, Belinda," Aimee said briskly, sweeping into the kitchen with a tray full of dirty dishes. "Are you talking about that silly legend again? People in this town are obsessed with it. I don't even think there was a real Evangeline at all. It's all a made-up story designed to bring in the tourists."

Belinda's brow furrowed and she sent a dark look in Aimee's direction. "That legend is as true as you and me standing here. Many folks even swear that they've seen her ghost wandering the hills, calling for her long-lost—"

"Fools and drunkards," Aimee interrupted, sending an exasperated look in my direction as if she expected for me to side with her.

"I think I've dreamt of her twice now," I said slowly. "Both times it felt so real that I wasn't sure whether or not I was dreaming."

There was silence while both of them stared at me.

Belinda shook her head and smiled. "Well, of course, you'd dream of her while you're staying at Dark Lady Farm, especially with her being a relative and all. The whole place is crawling with paintings, sculptures, and assorted artwork of her. I bet we've all dreamed of her at one point or another. Haven't we, Aimee?"

Aimee stared at me thoughtfully ... "No, I can't say that I

have," she said slowly. "But there are others who dream of her quite regularly. They say that dreams of the Dark Lady are prophetic; they show the dreamer how the future will unfold."

She stared at me steadily until I looked away with a shiver, remembering how things had been in my dream.

"Have you had a tour of the house, dear?" Belinda asked. "We used to give proper guided tours to tourists at least twice a year. I do miss that. I know this house top to bottom."

"I don't think she needs a tour *now*," Aimee said in exasperation. "She doesn't care about the history of this drafty old house. Xan and Estelle had lunch in the garden, but I heard them say that they'd be headed to the stables next. I'm sure you'd much prefer to be outside in the fresh air with them."

"Oh no, I'd love to see the house," I said eagerly, smiling at Belinda. "I'm fascinated by history. Plus, it would help if I knew my way around. I nearly got lost this morning."

"Excellent. I'll leave the dishes until we get back then. Come along."

I followed closely after Belinda as she marched from the kitchen, through the foyer, and back down the hall to where my room was situated. Aimee trailed a few feet behind, a sulky look on her face.

"We'll start right at the beginning for you, so you don't get lost again. You've probably already guessed that this is the guest wing. Ruth has kept it much the same as it was back in her own great, great grandfather's day. You know your room, of course, and each of these is done in a similar theme, though in a different colour. Here, we'll poke our heads in a few of them just to give you an idea but they're very much—"

She set her hand on a doorknob a few doors down from my room and then broke off with a sharp cry as Morris fled out and shot down the hallway out of sight, his tail puffed up and his green eyes wide with indignation.

"Now, how on earth did you get in there, you scoundrel?"

she called after him and shook her head. "That's a puzzle; these doors are hardly ever opened."

I flushed beet red and was just about to confess that I'd done a bit of earlier exploring when I saw Aimee watching me closely with what could only be a look of brooding suspicion on her face. I smiled at her weakly and chose to say nothing.

I pretended to be interested as Belinda told me all about the fabric on the beds and the make of the antique tables, but my mind was wondering about that strange look I'd seen on Aimee's face. Why would it matter so much if I poked around a little? Nobody was even staying in these rooms and it wasn't as if I'd stolen anything.

"Most of these paintings are of your ancestors, dear. Some of them were quite famous, as you probably know."

She pointed to a grey-haired man wearing a high collar, his blue, slightly-crossed eyes staring dreamily off into the distance. "This one is your Great, Great Uncle Herbert who had a hand in designing the pickle grabber."

"Pardon me?"

"Oh, you know, that spiky claw-like thing that grabs pickles out of the jar. He invented that, or something similar to it. Surely you know that story."

"Mother never mentioned it," I said, pressing my lips together to suppress my laughter. I had a feeling that Mother would have rather been tossed off a high building than admit to being related to a pickle-grabbing inventor.

"And here's Mad Edna—I can't remember how she'd be related to you dear—who was locked up by her husband for communing with spirits. It was probably just an excuse to steal her inheritance and marry someone else; it was a rather common practice in those days, I'm afraid. That's how Aimee's distantly related, aren't you Mad Edna's descendant, dear?"

I was certain that she hadn't meant it rudely, but Aimee's face went beet red and her eyes glittered with angry tears.

"Oh, I didn't know you were a cousin of mine, Aimee, that's wonderful," I said quickly, trying to be kind.

She turned her gaze on me, and it was all I could do to keep from taking a few steps back at the barely concealed fury in her eyes.

"Distant," she said, taking a few short breaths to calm herself. "Very, very distant. Now if you'll excuse me, I have chores to finish."

She scuttled away; her shoulders hunched as if she were carrying a heavy burden.

"Oh, never mind that one," Belinda said, frowning after the young maid. "She's always getting caught up in some drama or another. She was such a sweet, meek thing when she first came to the house, too. She's a far-off cousin, and an orphan, so Ruth of course did the right thing and took her on when she turned up on the doorstep looking for a job. Ruth hired her to do light work around the house and even insisted that Aimee finish her high school diploma.

"Ever since she met that boyfriend of hers, though, she's not content with what she has; she's gotten all these wild ideas above her station in life. I told her she should just be grateful for a roof over her head, but she didn't think much of that, I can tell you."

No, I imagine not, I thought, feeling sorry for Aimee. *Belinda's a little old-fashioned to be talking about people staying in their stations in life. That's something Mother would say.*

I followed Belinda through the rest of the tour for what ended up being the most interesting family history lesson I'd ever had. I'd never dreamed that I had so many criminals, mad inventors, and thieving scoundrels in my past but apparently, I came from a long line of brilliant but borderline murderous ancestors. Mother had overlooked whole branches of my family tree when she was busy telling me to be more ladylike so I could do the family credit.

When Belinda finally paused for breath, I asked the question that had most bothered me. "Where did all the paintings and figurines of Evangeline come from, though? Some of them don't look that old."

"Oh, some of them came from your ancestors over the years. Your Great, Great Grandfather Alocious had the stained-glass window made. And your Great Aunt Ruth herself has gathered a huge collection of the smaller pieces. One of her greatest passions is to add to her stock. She swears they'll be worth a lot of money one day. Dark Lady souvenirs do a brisk trade in the village and there are a few talented local artists around. She brings home new pieces at least once a month and some she has specially commissioned. Besides the horses, they are her pride and joy.

We paused at the end of the hall where the stained-glass window stood and I regarded it warily, glad that the dog had at least stayed in its original position this time.

"This, of course, is the house's crowning glory. It took over a year for the artists to make it. Alocious designed every bit of it himself and oversaw the installation. He was very proud of it. Now, if you'll just follow me back here."

She ushered us behind the stairs where a set of large doors that I'd somehow overlooked stood open.

"This is the ballroom and it also served as a dining room for the larger dinner parties. We, of course, have a smaller dining room as well for when the guest list had less than forty people. This house has seen its share of galas, I can tell you."

"Amazing," I said, taking in the huge expanse of highly polished wooden floor. It was designed in a half-circle and the far side was all curved windows with built-in seating beneath them. When Belinda flicked a switch, the chandeliers overhead danced with a thousand lights. Not one, but two large grand pianos stood in the far corner on a raised stage. I could imagine all the shoes that must have danced across that floor in the last few hundred years.

"You can almost hear the music of those bygone times," Belinda said, her eyes sparkling. "Oh, how I wish I could have been there when the house was in its glory days. It must have been magnificent. Your Great Aunt Ruth isn't one for parties and socializing. She prefers a quiet life. I always hoped I'd see the day when a new heir would sweep in and restore the place to the way it was before. Can you imagine?"

"Yes," I agreed, glancing over at her rapt expression as she stared around the empty ballroom with her hands clasped reverently in front of her. "It must have been quite something." Secretly, though, I was with Ruth on this one; I would much prefer to read a book or be out in the barn over going to parties and talking to strangers.

"Oh, you must think I'm a sentimental old lady." She laughed and patted me on the arm. "But I love this beautiful old house. It has its own personality and I know it would love to see its old glory days restored."

After that, we saw the less formal dining room and the breakfast room, a small room for playing billiards, and a half dozen sitting rooms for various purposes that I couldn't fathom. In the back, there was the kitchen, laundry and a mudroom, Belinda's suite and servants' quarters with rooms for Aimee, Estelle, and Jacob.

That's funny, I thought as Belinda pointed out Jacob's closed door. *I swear that Aimee ran upstairs to get his medication. And then she led him upstairs once he was feeling better, too. Why would he have two rooms?*

I didn't have too much time to think about it because Belinda was leading me back to the kitchen and toward a set of narrow stairs that led upward from the servant's quarters.

"Oh, I think we've taken quite enough of Jillian's time," Aimee said loudly, appearing behind us. "Besides, Ruth always said the upstairs is closed to tours, we shouldn't take anyone up there."

Belinda turned and the two of them locked eyes in some sort of staring contest, which Aimee, by sheer willpower, somehow won.

"Oh, fine," Belinda said, huffing in irritation. "Actually, there is one more room down here I haven't shown you. I don't know why I didn't think of it right away. Betty told me what a bookish young thing you were when you were a child. "Come this way."

She led me back almost to the big entryway and opened a small door on the left, so unobtrusive that it looked just like a door to a narrow closet.

"Oh," I said, clapping my hands together in amazement like a little kid. "It's fantastic."

"There, you see, I thought you'd like it. This was your great, great grandfather's private library. Ruth uses this one sometimes, too, but she has her own, cozier, one upstairs for everyday use. You can visit here as often as you like."

"I love it," I said breathlessly, looking around at the towering stacks of leather-bound books rising all around me from floor to ceiling. It was a big room but didn't feel imposing. It had plush chairs and a fireplace and a thick carpet on the floor. A big display cabinet stood in one corner, packed full of trophies and cups from various horse shows. On the very top shelf were more of those tiresome Dark Lady sculptures.

Dozens of photos of horses proudly posed with winning ribbons covered the far wall. Some were faded with age and some were quite new. Great Aunt Ruth knew how to breed some top-class horses.

The adjoining wall had a different theme; paintings, and old black and white photos of barns and rolling landscapes covered the entire surface, and I went closer to inspect them.

"Those are all of Dark Lady Farm at different points in

history. See, this was what the barn looked like before the renovations."

"Oh," I said, studying the photo she'd pointed at. It was an old sepia-coloured photo showing the interior of a much smaller barn. The stone wasn't crumbling, it looked newer and better kept. Sleek horses looked out over the stall doors, pricking their ears for the camera.

"That one looks just like the little colt I met," I laughed, looking at the awkwardly disproportioned yearling in the last stall.

"And this painting here shows what it looked like at a much earlier time."

It looked pretty much the same as the pre-renovation photo except for the bright whitewash on the stone and the grooms wearing funny-looking clothes who stood near the horses' heads. This time a bold-looking red horse stood in the colt's stall, his eyes staring out of the painting with a commanding air.

I narrowed my eyes at him. He looked strangely familiar, but Belinda started talking again before I could ask about him.

"There are all sorts of books in here, some of them were even written by your ancestors. After dinner, you'll have to curl up in here and we'll light a fire and you can do some exploring."

"Thank you," I said, truly delighted. "I'd like nothing better. But right now, I better head out to the barn. They're probably waiting for me."

"Of course, dear, run along," Belinda said. "We'll see you at supper."

I thanked Belinda for my tour, and then headed out to the barn, a little annoyed with myself for leaving Bally grazing alone by himself for so long while I was enjoying exploring the house. He was a steady, dependable horse, but he was still my responsibility and I'd never forgive myself if anything happened to him.

He wasn't where I left him, but I heard voices and laughter coming from the big indoor arena behind the stable area.

The door was open and I tip-toed inside carefully, not wanting to startle whatever horses were in the ring. I needn't have worried, though, because Gil was riding Bally at the far end and Xan was casually seated on an elegant bay horse, his reins bunched in one hand while he waved the other one around to illustrate some funny story he was entertaining Estelle with.

"And then ... and then I just told him ..." He laughed, hardly able to finish and then broke off when he saw me. "Jilly! You're just in time to see me ride. Estelle's been generous enough to split the horses between me and your stable boy there, so there should be plenty to entertain you with."

"It was hardly me being generous," Estelle said, "you're both doing me a huge favour by exercising the horses at all. I don't know what I would have done if you three hadn't have shown up. I'm sorry we were so rude to you earlier; we're very protective of Ruth and she's spoken strongly about not trusting her relatives before. Clearly, she didn't mean you, though, especially since you say she sent you a letter to come to visit, Xan."

She batted her eyes at him and his cheeks flushed pink.

"Don't worry about it, most of our relatives are completely nuts," Xan said firmly. "I don't blame old Ruthless, I mean, Great Aunt Ruth one bit."

Estelle looked a little startled at the nickname, but regained her composure quickly, beaming up at Xan with shining eyes. It was weird how quickly those two had hit it off, especially with the way Xan teased me so mercilessly about having Gil as a best friend. Estelle worked in a stable just like Gil but that didn't seem to faze Xan one bit.

"Hey, are you planning to exercise that horse or just stand

there and look pretty," Gil said, cruising past with Bally in a ground-covering extended trot.

Xan gritted his teeth and wheeled the dark bay around, causing the animal to jump sideways in surprise.

"Easy on his mouth," Estelle said sharply, gripping the top board of the arena tightly in both hands until her knuckles turned white, "he's sensitive."

Xan loosened his reins immediately and gave the bay a cursory pat on the neck, shooting a glare at Gil's retreating back. "Sorry," he said, "I'm still getting used to him."

After that, he rode more cautiously, ignoring Gil and taking time to figure out how to give the horse underneath him a good ride. The large animal moved with big, powerful strides across the ring but his mouth was light on the bit and I could see Xan's face light up when he realized that he could communicate with him with the barest of touches.

"That's great," Estelle called, "he's listening to you now."

She sighed deeply, caught my glance and smiled ruefully. "Isn't it awful when you first let other people ride your horses? I always feel like I'm sending an unprepared child off with a stranger."

"I know what you mean," I said because that was the way I felt whenever one of the sale horses I'd trained left our stables. But I didn't feel that way right now; watching Gil ride Bally was a pleasure and I never doubted for a single second that my horse was in the best of hands.

"That horse is Baron, one of my favourites. You probably met him in the woods that night after I fell off. I've been with him since he was a baby. He was born here."

"He's lovely," I said, watching Xan work the horse in a smooth serpentine pattern back and forth across the ring. Xan loved being outside, galloping fast and jumping anything in his path; doing ring work wasn't his thing but his forehead was furrowed in concentration and he looked like he was giving it his all.

"Yes," Estelle sighed heavily. "I'd do anything to buy him."

Her voice trembled a little and I looked over to see her lower lip quivering.

"Oh, I'm sorry. Is he for sale?"

"They're all for sale," Estelle said, regaining her composure, "for the right price, that is. But Ruthie, er, your Great Aunt Ruth, has held on to him the longest … probably for my sake. The thing is that he's so talented; I'm a decent rider, but he's got the ability to jump the really big fences and I don't. He's world-class and I'm, well, just average."

"I doubt that. Great Aunt Ruth wouldn't keep you here riding her horses if you were just average."

"I'm talented, I suppose, but I'm not brave enough when the fences get much over four feet. Even the thought of riding the higher courses makes me ill. Still, I'll hate to see him go. He and I have a special bond."

I watched Xan and the big horse thoughtfully. Xan was fearless but his coaches were always bothering him about his lack of discipline; he acted like he was allergic to hard work sometimes and he pretty much expected his horses to perform well without him schooling them consistently. Maybe, if he put his mind to it, he could be the second rider that Ruth and Estelle needed. Maybe that's why Ruth had sent him the letter in the first place.

Gil and Xan rode five horses each, including Rigel, who only pulled a few tricks this time, and by the end, both riders were both red-faced with exertion. And we still had to bring everyone in from the pasture and feed them.

Estelle sat on a hay bale in the aisle with her crutches tucked beside her, reminding us where to put each horse as we led them in one by one and got them tucked away in their stalls.

She'd already assured me that she would appreciate any grooming or ground-work I could do with the horses so, after I'd collected little Damascus from his field, I grabbed a box of brushes and slipped back into his stall.

He looked surprised that someone was paying attention to him and was very interested in the grooming kit. He gently picked up each brush and held it between his little teeth for a second, bobbing his nose up and down playfully as he tasted each one.

"You are adorable," I told him, as I worked a curry comb over his fuzzy coat. When I was a child, Mother had tried to force me to let the grooms get all my horses ready so I wouldn't get so dirty all the time, but right from the beginning, I had rebelled. It was true that as a teenager I hadn't put my foot down very often but, where the horses were concerned, I was stubborn and somehow usually managed to get my way. Spending time with them was blissful and getting dirty had never bothered me one bit.

The colt's spiky little black mane stood straight up the air and I did my best to smooth it to one side, laughing when it popped right back up again like it had a mind of its own.

"Do you remember how to pick up your feet?" I asked gently, frowning when I noticed his pint-sized hooves were overdue for a trim. I slid my hand lightly down the inside of his leg and waited for a few beats for him to respond. He lifted his foot abruptly and held it way up in the air, wobbling on his unaccustomed three legs.

"Good boy," I said, picking the dirt out of the tiny hoof swiftly and returning it to the ground before he could fall on me.

I laughed at his astonished expression and scratched him in that nice spot behind his ear that most horses seemed to love. He sniffed the hoof pick carefully and then let me lift and clean his back foot, and then the two on the other side. I went slowly with him, giving him lots of time to find his balance. I had the feeling that he was the type of horse that would need lots of patience and encouragement at each stage in his training. Some horses could be rushed through the process and turn out relatively unscathed, but more sensitive souls could be easily ruined by thoughtless handling.

As I slid out of the stall, I realized that a conversation had been going on while I was occupied.

"I thought you said she'd be back in a few weeks," Gil said, his voice strangely flat.

"Oh," Estelle said nervously, "a few weeks or a month. She bought an open-ended ticket so it might be a bit sooner or a bit later."

"And you said she was in Florida?"

There was a long pause. "No, not Florida, France. She's doing a tour of Europe and visiting some relatives along the way."

"Oh, which ones?" Xan asked with interest. "I stayed in Prague a few years ago with some sort of cousins. They were very strange; they'd only wear black and took me to the ghastliest restaurants. I was a bit relieved to come home, quite frankly."

"I really couldn't say," Estelle said sharply. "Ruth doesn't share every last detail with me."

"But surely you have a way to contact her if there's an emergency," Gil insisted, "or have some idea of her travel plans. The phone must be working by now."

"Oh, yes, of course, it is," Estelle said hastily. "Ruth left us a travel itinerary in her office but I can't be expected to remember everything on it right now, can I? I'm so sorry, Xan, but I'm feeling a little lightheaded. Would you be able to help me get back to the house?"

"Of course," Xan said, shooting a dark look at Gil, "here, lean on me, I'll help you."

"Well, that was interesting," Gil said, watching Estelle hobble away with Xan carefully hovering over her. Apparently, he'd forgotten our argument before lunch and was speaking to me again.

"What was? Why were you interrogating the poor girl?"

"I am sure that earlier Aimee told me that Ruth was in Florida."

"Did she? I don't remember. Are you sure that's what she said?"

"No, I guess not a hundred percent." Gil frowned. "I just feel that things aren't quite right here. I can't see anyone in this day and age not fixing faulty phone lines when there's no cell service."

"I don't know, if Great Aunt Ruth is eccentric as my mother then I could see her being too cheap or stubborn to fix things. She's not a fan of technology at the best of times."

This was an understatement. Our manor was only a tiny bit more modern than Dark Lady Farm. We had cell phones and there was internet in the barn and my parent's office but that was about it. Mother wouldn't even have a radio in the house let alone a television. Something about the noise disturbing her.

"True," Gil said, cracking a smile. Probably thinking about how many times had I snuck over to his house to listen to music or watch movies.

"The horses look fantastic anyway. How were they to ride?"

"Good. They've been schooled with a very light hand, which says something about their training program anyway. There are a few there that would make some nice prospects. You should tell your mother."

"I doubt she'd buy anything from Great Aunt Ruth; they've always been at odds with one another. I'd like to take that colt home, though."

"The little bay? Hard to say how he'll turn out."

"I'd place my bets on him turning out to be something special. I wonder how much she'd ask for him."

"Probably more than the two of us have combined, even if he is ugly right now."

"He's lovely, not ugly," I protested. But you're probably right."

I sighed. Despite living in a mansion, riding the most expensive horses money could buy, and having travelled around the world several times, I still had very little access to capital. Mother controlled the purse strings in our household like a vengeful dragon guarding its hoard, and the only money I had of my own was a small portion of the prize money I'd earned at shows. Besides riding full-time, I'd never actually had a job or made any money on my own. Bally had been a birthday present from Father so I owned him outright, but I was well aware that everything else in my life could be taken away at just a moment's notice.

"I could probably ask Father for a loan if it's something I really wanted," I said slowly. "But I don't like asking him for favours since it usually throws Mother into a temper for weeks. Then we all suffer."

"Yes, she's something, isn't she?"

We walked in silence and then Gil said, "Jilly, wouldn't it be nice if we could go away somewhere and open our own barn? If we could get some start-up capital, I'm sure we could attract the right sort of clients. We both have proven show records."

"That's impossible, Gil," I said without even thinking. It wasn't the first time he'd asked me or even the tenth time, and no matter what I said, he never seemed to understand why it wouldn't work.

Why wouldn't it work? A tiny voice in my head whispered. And for the first time in a long time, I paused and examined the question properly. We didn't have any money for one thing.

How would we live? Where would we find work? The idea of leaving Greystone was beyond terrifying, but still, I felt a tiny shiver of interest. Things always seemed so damned *possible* when I was around Gil.

"Come on," he said encouragingly, seeing the expression on my face waver. "Don't you remember when we were kids and we talked about having our own barn together where we could train the horses just like we wanted without our parents interfering? We drew up the blueprints and had a business plan and everything. We were going to ask your dad to sponsor us."

"Were we?" I asked, frowning as I struggled to remember. A dim memory floated to the surface of the two of us lying on our bellies in the hayloft with notebooks scattered around us, chattering excitedly while we carefully designing our dream barn.

"Yes," Gil said firmly, "we did. It wasn't that long ago, Jilly, and we talked about it all the time. Why can't you remember that?"

"I'm not sure, Gil," I said gently, "I believe you, but we were kids. I'm sure we made all sorts of plans. How can I be expected to remember every detail?"

"Because you made me swear that I wouldn't let you forget," he said, turning to me, his voice almost a growl, "right before you got sick you said that our plans to leave were the only things that kept you hanging on and that I shouldn't let you forget them."

The raw hurt in his eyes nearly brought me to tears.

"I'm so sorry," I whispered. "I know there is something wrong with me. I don't remember the same things you do. When I got sick, I lost things. You know that. It was that fever, I think. I'm not trying to hurt you, Gil. But, I'm not unhappy at Greystone. I don't see any reason to leave."

This was not quite true but it was easier than telling him how truly terrified I was to leave the safety of my home. To go out into the world to face a sea of people who might mock and torment me.

"That's the problem," Gil said quietly, "the old Jilly would have seen lots of reasons. She was fierce and fearless and she would have never have been blind enough to let her awful mother push someone like Frederick on her."

"That's not fair," I said, feeling stung. "And I don't like this conversation anymore. Let's talk about something else instead. Something more pleasant."

Gil sighed heavily and rubbed a hand over his eyes. "I can't do this any longer," he said, his voice thick with emotion.

Something in his tone sent a jolt of fear through me and I reached out instinctively and put a hand on his arm.

"Do what?" I whispered, my heart beating rapidly. *Don't leave, don't leave, don't leave*, I chanted silently, fearing the worst, knowing that this day might come eventually.

He looked into my eyes a long time, guessing my thoughts. "I can't stay at Greystone forever, Jilly," he said finally. "I'm suffocating there and I can't stand around and watch you throw away the rest of your life." He held up a hand to cut off my protest. "I've spent too long waiting for the old Jilly to come back and I've about given up; I can't do it any longer. Someday soon, I'm going to do something different in my life than work for your harpy of a mother. And you'll have to decide whether you want to come with me or not. Because when I leave, I won't be coming back."

He kicked at the ground violently and then strode off in the direction of the house without a backward glance.

I stood there staring after him, my head throbbing and my throat clogged with tears. There was a deep and terrible sadness in my heart, a feeling of loss that eclipsed anything I'd felt for awful-Frederick. There was a small thump against the heel of my boot and I looked down to see Morris standing with one paw on my foot, rubbing his heavy head against my left shin, a blissful look on his face.

"Oh, Morris," I said, my tears finally finding their outlet.

I reached down and scooped him up, holding him tight against my chest as I cried into his soft fur. He didn't squirm away; he just broke into a deep, comforting purr.

By the time I'd reached my room, washed my face and changed into dinner clothes the emotions I'd felt earlier had faded to a more comfortable level and I'd managed to compose myself. I wasn't even sure what all the fuss had been about.

"I think Gil's being very silly over nothing, Morris," I told the big cat. "Why should anything have to change? We can just keep things exactly as they are forever."

Pondering, I made my way slowly down the hall to where dinner was waiting.

Chapter 7

Dinner was a strangely formal affair that evening. Instead of serving us in our rooms, Belinda and Aimee had set out the dining room table properly and we gathered around in the stiff, high-backed chairs and ate a six-course meal fit for royalty.

I was surprised when Jacob and Estelle, and then Aimee and Belinda, found spaces for themselves at the table and sat down as naturally as could be. Not that I minded, of course, but I'd have thought that Great Aunt Ruthless would have been a stickler for the rule that the help ate somewhere else out of sight.

"We run a strange house here," Belinda said, catching my eye. "Ruth had her ideas and I suspect that she was often lonely. She decided long ago that mealtimes were when everyone would gather and discuss the running of the house together. She always insisted that we were a team and that Dark Lady Farm was the master of us all, not herself."

"*Is*," Estelle corrected quickly, "you meant to say Ruth *is*."

"Of course, I did," Belinda coughed, looked down at her plate and took a large bite of chicken.

Xan and Estelle sat close together, talking quietly to themselves and practically ignoring everyone else, their heads nearly touched as they laughed over some private joke.

Watching Xan and Estelle so cozy together sent a little pang of longing through my chest. Once upon a time that had been Gil and me, lost in our own little world. And then it had been Frederick and me. And then nobody.

I caught Gil watching me from across the table and knew he'd guess my glum thoughts, but as soon as I smiled tentatively, he looked away and struck up a conversation with Belinda beside him.

After that, it was a silent meal for me. I ate the delicious food, wrapped up in my own thoughts and listening half-heartedly to the conversation around me.

Belinda suggested that everyone retire to one of the little sitting rooms for dessert and coffee, and I thought that maybe this was my chance to slip away and go mope in my room alone for a while. Maybe Morris would be there to curl up with me.

"Now, don't run away so quickly," Belinda said quietly, coming up behind me just as I was heading down the hallway. "You just come along to the library; I have something to show you."

"I was just going to my room to rest," I said, "I think I might have a headache coming on."

"I expect that will clear up once you've had a moment to yourself. If you don't mind, I'd also like to have a quick word with you," Belinda said. "Alone."

"Oh, all right." I shrugged and followed her down the hall.

We went through the little hidden door into the library and found Aimee already kneeling on the hearth lighting a fire.

"It gets cold in here," she said brusquely, sending me an accusing look. "It would have been easier if you'd stayed with the others. Now I have to light two fires and bring your dessert and coffee all this way."

"Oh, you didn't have to …" I started to apologize.

"Never mind, it's done now," she snapped and bustled out without looking back.

"Don't pay any attention to that sour-puss," Belinda said. "Sit down, please. I'd like to say this to you while we're alone."

I sat down obediently near the fire and watched her expectantly, noticing how she twisted her fingers nervously together. What on earth could she possibly have to tell me?

"Now, you know I've been with this branch of your family a long time," Belinda said, waiting until I nodded before she went on again. "So, I know a little bit about what makes you people special."

"Special?" I said in surprise. "How so?"

"There's no need to be secretive about it," she said impatiently, glancing toward the door, "and we won't have much time alone together so I'd like to speak plainly now if you don't mind."

"Of course. Are you talking about making money with that Golden Touch thing? I'm pretty sure that's just a silly superstition. My theory is—"

Belinda cleared her throat loudly and gave me a stern look. "Young lady, this is not the time to be funny. I'm not saying I know how to explain it, but I'm well aware that almost every one of you is blessed with a unique gift."

"Um, okay," I said, a little taken back by her abrupt tone. She'd been much nicer earlier.

"Now, Betty has shared a little of what happened to you when you were young, how your gifts came early and were a bit too much for you to handle. She thought that with your special birthday coming up you might need some guidance and preparation than you've been given at home. I don't like to speak ill of anyone but that mother of yours—"

She stopped when she saw my blank expression.

"Belinda, I don't have the faintest clue what you're talking about," I said slowly. "Honestly, I have zero gifts or talents of any kind. Unless you count riding horses or failing at relationships." This last bit was my attempt at being funny but she didn't crack a smile.

She stared into my face; her expression worried.

"Oh, my dear, this is not good at all. I'll have to consult with Betty. Or perhaps the doctor will know what to do. Maybe your injury—" She wrung her hands together then stood up abruptly.

"Here, there isn't any time to waste." She went to one of the tall bookshelves, running her finger along the leather spines until she found what she was looking for.

"Jillian, whatever you may have been told, this family's gift is not about being good with money. It's that they've used their other talents to acquire that wealth. When they use that silly 'Golden Touch' phrase, it's a sort of catch-all that lumps all the individual abilities together. I suspect it's their way of being able to refer to it in public without anyone being suspicious.

"Here," she went on, ignoring my incredulous expression as she shoved the book into my hands, "I expect all your answers are in this book. Your Great, Great Grandfather Alocious wrote it. He had copies made for each of his children to pass down to their descendants. He was a very opinionated man, and I dare say that many of his ideas are horribly old-fashioned; he didn't fancy that women should do much of anything with their lives, for example. But he lays it out in a pretty straightforward way that I think you'll understand."

"Betty, I don't think—"

"Just read it," she snapped and then took a deep breath to calm herself. "Shall I see if the coffee is ready?"

"Um, okay," I said, shrinking back from her a little. Clearly, the woman was a bit unhinged and it would be best to humour her until I could escape to my room. I would read a few pages and then slip away when the coast was clear.

I ran my hand over the inky black cover. The book in my hands felt heavier than it should have for its small size and the leather had a strange, sinewy feel to it that I didn't much like. The title, *A Strange Family History*, was embossed on the cover with gold. I tried to flip it open to the first page and was surprised when it fell open instead to a spot in the middle of the book where the binding had been stretched. The chapter heading read: A False Gift of Elements and there was a line-drawing of a woman wearing an old-fashioned dress, balancing two towers of flame on each outstretched hand. The sketch was quite good, very life-like right down to the arrogant sneer on the woman's face. I frowned, noting a small burn mark in the upper right-hand corner of the old paper.

A false gift of elements? What on earth does that mean?

I flipped back to the beginning of the book and was surprised to see that it began with a two-column list, each with a heading. The first column had *True Gifts* written above it and the second column said *False Gifts*.

Precognition was the first item in the True column, followed by Clairvoyance, Telepathy, Dowsing, Prophecy, Psychometry and Astral Projection. There were more but I stopped there, shaking my head with disbelief. This seriously couldn't be what Belinda thought our Golden Touch was. I'd spent enough time with my crazy family to know that there was not a drop of magic between the lot of us. The idea of Mother using some sort of psychic gifts at all was laughable.

I glanced over at the False column and froze. Potions, Conjuration, Levitation, Divination ... the list went on, but it was the seventh one down that had caught my eye. Perception of Spirits.

Suddenly my stomach heaved. There was a pressing feeling in my skull like something wanted very badly to get out, and I clapped my hands against my temples and closed my eyes, waiting for the feeling to pass. It gradually faded and I stayed very, very still, holding my breath, overwhelmed by a strange feeling that I was no longer in my body. I don't know how long I would have stayed like that but for Belinda bustling into the room with a tray laden with coffee and dessert. I'd missed my chance to slip away.

"Oh, my dear," she said gently, setting the tray down. "Are you all right? Now you see what I was talking about, of course."

"No, no, I don't see anything," I said faintly. "I just feel a little strange. I might need to go lie down."

"Not quite yet," Belinda said firmly. "Hear me out first and then you can go rest. Betty had mentioned that you might be unprepared, but I didn't expect it to be this extreme."

"You spoke to her?" I asked. "I thought the phone was broken."

"Oh, it's all mended for now," she said quickly, "but it could go down again at any moment."

She didn't quite meet my eye when she said this and I felt certain she was lying. Right then, I wanted more than anything to find Gil and get out of here. He'd been right all along to be suspicious.

"Why does the book divide them into true and false gifts?" I asked, wiping my sweating palms against my jeans. I didn't want her to know how truly crazy I thought she was. There would be a better chance of escape if I played along.

"Well, your great, great grandfather was a peculiar man with some strange ideas about religion. I believe that the only way he could come to terms with the fact that his ancestors had gifts was to categorize them as good or bad. Good gifts he felt had been gifted by God and false gifts, I believe he thought came from the devil. It's all explained in there somewhere."

"So, some of these, so-called, gifts are bad?"

The Curse of The Golden Touch

"Your great, great grandfather thought so. But many others disagree. If you ask me, a gift is a gift. I just know that I would have given my eye teeth to have just one of them; any of them. Which brings me to my next question, dear; what is your gift?"

"Um …" I stared down at the book in my lap, my eyes scanning the true column for inspiration. Finally, I sighed. There was just no way I could pretend to believe any of this was more than superstitious nonsense. I couldn't do it.

"I'm sorry, I am completely giftless. Maybe it skipped a generation," I said hopefully, looking longingly toward the door.

"Nice try," Belinda said firmly, "here, if it makes you feel better, then you can just pretend for now that this is a made-up story you're writing. Betty said you were quite the writer when you were younger. If you were writing a story about a *very stubborn* girl who had a gift, one of the gifts on this list, then what would it be?"

I opened my mouth to say something flippant when the strange, pressing feeling in my head returned with a vengeance. I clapped my hands to my temples and shut my eyes as a rapid series of images flashed across the darkness of my mind. A young girl turning cartwheels across the grass, a ghostly terrier trotting at my heels, an old man in a rocking chair next to the stables. My kindly Nanny looking down at me so lovingly. And then I saw Mother's disappointed expression and the stern face of Dr. Crane looming over me, something silver and sharp in his hands. My eyes shot open.

"Perception of Spirits," I gasped loudly and then promptly burst into tears.

Chapter 8

It took Belinda over an hour to calm me down and get me to stop crying. She said kind things and brought me tea and wrapped me in a blanket and patted my shoulder ineffectually but nothing helped. Even though I knew I was being hysterical I just couldn't seem to find a way to make myself quit.

Finally, I came to an exhausted, hiccupping stop on my own and wiped my swollen eyes on a corner of the blanket.

"I'm so sorry," I said, sniffling. "I have no idea what came over me."

She laid a hand on my arm, looking nearly as sad as I felt. "No, I'm the one who needs to apologize, dear. I'm sorry for what you lost and for the part of the past that I thoughtlessly dredged up. I thought you must have known all about it by now. It's always a bad business when gifts are tampered with. It's a horrible, outdated practice."

"But why?"

"Well," she said slowly, "unfortunately, it's more common in your particular family than in others. Your ancestor Alocious became quite the expert in removing 'undesirable' gifts from his descendants. I mentioned that he had very strong opinions on many things: he believed that the gifts were there solely to bring financial prosperity. Any gift that he couldn't see the use for, especially in the female family members, he felt should be removed in order to make way for better ones. It also often has the, ahem, side-effect, of making the patient more obedient and easier to influence afterward. Very useful for taming rebellious children."

"No," I said, clapping a hand over my mouth. "I don't believe it." But suddenly I did believe it. Very much. I could perfectly envision Mother doing something like this.

"It's a very outdated practice now," Belinda said sadly, "but it's still used at a parent's discretion. A baby is often born with the potential for multiple gifts and it's felt that if an undesirable gift is removed that it allows the others to flourish."

I sat there feeling wounded and lost, my stomach roiling around like a small raft on a stormy sea.

"But how?" I asked.

Belinda sighed heavily. "Oh, it's a mixture of electroshock treatment and hypnotism I suppose. I hear it's painless, though; the patients are sedated. They don't even remember it afterward."

"The *children*, you mean? It's done on innocent kids who don't have a choice, right?"

She nodded unhappily. "Mostly children and a few adults who have ... issues with their gifts."

I felt truly sick now, like any second I'd throw up all over this nice carpet.

"I have to go," I said, pulling myself out of the chair and heading toward the door. This time Belinda didn't try and stop me.

"Just one more question," I said, pausing in the doorway. "Can it be reversed? Can it be undone?"

She didn't answer right away but her sorrowful expression

told me everything I needed to know and I turned and fled into the night.

I didn't stop until I reached the safety of Bally's stall. He nickered sleepily as I came in. I ran my hand down his silky neck and then stumbled to the far corner of his stall where I crumpled against the wall. I didn't cry, I was all cried out; I just stared at the wooden boards and let my thoughts tumble over each other. Bally pushed some of his hay over to where I was sitting and ate with his nose next to my knee, reaching out occasionally to blow his warm breath on my cheek.

I almost didn't hear when the door slid back and Gil walked softly inside. I wanted to look up, to say something, but I just didn't have the energy to move.

He stared at me a long while and then came over and sat down close beside me. I let myself lean into him and he reached over and took both of my cold hands in his warm one.

"Belinda said I should come and find you. Are you okay?" he asked softly and I wanted to assure him brightly that yes, of course I was okay, like I usually would, but this time I just couldn't do it. I finally shook my head and he squeezed my fingers a little tighter.

"Do you want me to stay?" This time, after a slight hesitation, I nodded and he wrapped his free arm around my shoulders and tucked me in close beside him.

We were silent for a long time.

"Gil," I said finally, in a voice I didn't recognize. "You should leave Greystone. You should get away from there as fast as possible. Don't wait for me. I'm broken and I don't think I can ever be fixed."

I waited dully for him to get up and leave but instead, he just pulled me closer and rested his chin on my head.

"We're a team, Jilly," he said quietly. "Best friends. Where you go, I go."

That nearly started the tears all over again. A part of me wanted to tell him everything I'd learned that night but I didn't know where to begin. And I was exhausted. Instead, I inhaled deeply and closed my eyes, soothed by the steady, familiar beating of his heart.

Chapter 9

It was late when I'd stumbled into bed, exhausted, and I expected to pass out and not wake up until noon the next day. But my body and mind had other ideas. I must have slept for a little while but my eyes opened abruptly in the darkness and I looked over at the dresser clock to see that it was only three in the morning. I was wide awake and there was no point in lying there and staring at the ceiling.

Sighing, I threw back my covers and rolled out of bed. I threw on my robe and slippers and, yawning, made my way down the half-lit hall to the library. I still felt queasy and uncertain about what I'd discovered last night but I was also determined to know everything. And that started with reading the rest of that awful book from cover to cover.

Morris met me in the dimly lit hallway at the foot of the stairs and chirped a good morning at me on his way past me to the kitchen where Belinda had been leaving him bowls of cream and bits of diced meat.

"Well, you've certainly made yourself comfortable," I said as he trotted by with his tail in the air. "Don't get too used to it, you'll have to go right back to being a barn cat when we get home."

I paused, frowning unhappily. Was there any reason that *any* of us had to go back to Greystone? Gil might be willing to risk us starting on our own without money or a plan but I wasn't quite so adventurous.

We don't have anything to live on, I thought, pushing open the half-hidden library door and slipping inside. *And I'd need to board Bally somewhere and find work somehow. I've never even held a job before.*

I wondered briefly if Great Aunt Ruth would just let us stay here until we figured out what to do and then pushed the thought away. It was Xan she liked, not me and Gil, and I doubted that she'd risk an all-out feud with Mother to help us.

The book was on the table where I'd left it. I eyed the sinewy black cover distastefully then picked it up quickly before I could change my mind.

I kicked off my slippers and curled my feet up underneath me in the chair, tucking the edges of my robe around them. I wished that I'd thought to start a fire in the hearth first.

There was a soft throw draped over the chair and I pulled it around my shoulders. Still, I didn't open the book. I looked around me instead, studying the details of the nearby paintings. My gaze was caught by the painting of the red horse in the old Dark Lady stables. He looked very much like the horse the Lady had ridden in my dream. He stared so intently at me that it was almost hard to look away.

I could almost imagine that he's trying to tell me something, I thought uncomfortably then resolutely opened the book on my lap and began to read.

Even though I reluctantly believed what Belinda had told me last night I still found the book to be pretty unbelievable. I mean, magic powers and paranormal abilities? I couldn't envision my mother being telepathic or tromping out on the hills dowsing for water.

Also, it was clear that the author, my ancestor Alocious, had been a rotten human being. He'd managed to be sexist, racist, and elitist all in one delusional package. He'd made it clear that, in his opinion, the women in the family couldn't be trusted to manage their powers or their own money, without his expert guidance. Gross.

I'd made it through the first five chapters when a slight, squeaking noise in the doorway made me look up.

"Morris?" I asked uncertainly as the door inched inward until a faint sliver of lamp-light showed from the hallway.

There was no response, but a second later I heard faint voices headed toward me.

"Is it done?" a low masculine voice growled.

"Yes, almost. I'm working on it, I promise. I know I can find the last of them soon. We're so close."

I was sure the breathless response was Aimee's but the other voice was too low for me to recognize.

"Our time's almost up," the voice said, "don't disappoint me again."

"Oh, I won't, I won't," Aimee said anxiously. "Do you have to go so soon? I hardly ever see you anymore…"

"Don't cling. I've warned you…" His muttered voice faded away into a low grumble as they headed down the hall.

Poor Aimee, I thought, *I hope that's not the boyfriend she mentioned. But who else would be leaving here at four in the morning? What an unpleasant-sounding man. Whatever they were talking about, it sounded serious.*

I went back to my book, half-listening for the sound of the heavy front door opening and closing behind the visitor. So I nearly jumped out of my skin when I happened to look up and found Aimee staring at me from the open doorway with flushed cheeks and narrowed eyes, a calculating look on her face.

"Aimee," I gasped, putting a hand over my heart, "good grief you scared me."

She shook herself as if coming awake and bared her teeth in an insincere smile. "I didn't expect you to be up so early. What are you doing in here?"

"Homework," I said, holding the book up so she could see the cover. "I have some family history to catch up on."

"Oh, ug, *that* book," she said, wrinkling her nose. "Alocious was awful. I'm glad my side of the family didn't fall for that nonsense. I was always encouraged to embrace all my gifts unlike some poor—"

She broke off and looked away, her cheeks flushing a deeper shade of red.

"So, you have more than one gift then?" I asked politely, wondering if it had been me that she was about to confess feeling sorry for. I wasn't offended, the whole thing felt like I was in a dream. Who could have imagined a week ago that I'd be having a serious conversation about extrasensory abilities and powers with a cousin I'd never heard of? Life certainly knew how to throw some fantastic curveballs. And apparently, my entire existence had been built on secrets and lies.

"Well," she said tentatively, coming further into the room and shutting the door tightly behind her, "I don't like to brag but I can show you this …"

She held her arms away from her sides with her palms up. Without any warning at all, two little twin columns of fire erupted, one in the center of each hand.

"Oh, Aimee," I yelped, caught between fear and fascination, "that's amazing."

"That's just parlour tricks," she said, laughing. She clapped her palms together and then casually tossed a ball of flame into the fireplace where it instantly lit the stack of wood into a cheerfully crackling blaze.

"Now, your turn," she said, dropping into the seat next to me with a mischievous grin. She looked relaxed and happy for the first time since I'd met her.

I think we could be friends eventually, I thought in surprise. Wanting to spend more time with strangers wasn't something that I felt often.

"Oh, I can't do anything like that,' I said quickly, "I think my one talent is gone."

"Sorry, I heard about the ghost removal thing; that's too bad, it could have been useful. But you got some gift all right, a big thunderstorm of a gift whirling around inside of you, just waiting to get out."

I sat up, eyes widening in surprise. "Inside me? I don't feel anything. How do you know?"

She shrugged. "I'm not sure, I just do; it's something I can sense in people. Just like I know that Xan hasn't any gifts at all. Besides, even if I couldn't sense it, I would still guess that you had a big gift, what with your mother being so powerful and everything."

"My mother?" I said in astonishment. "How do you know?"

"Come on, everyone knows that. Your mom has some crazy abilities to see the future. She's better at it than anyone in the last hundred years."

Oh, so that explains why we're so rich then, if she can see the outcome of every business move. I thought glumly. *She's a total cheater. Nobody would stand a chance against her.*

Still, she hadn't saved me from nearly drowning in the Greystone River when I was a teenager, and she hadn't saved me from loving Frederick. So, she couldn't be as powerful as everyone thought she was.

Unless she didn't want to save me from those things. The thought came to me unbidden. My skin felt cold and clammy and I fought back a wave of nausea.

I thought back to every skinned knee and taunt from school children, I thought back to the year when Xan and his siblings became orphaned. Nobody had reached out to help their parents when they were in financial distress and almost nobody had stepped forward to help the children, either. And, if she was so powerful, then she *could* have. She could have given them the advice they needed to save their estate, their assets and their family. She could have stopped their parents from dying.

I looked down, realizing I was clenching the book hard between my hands. I let go and it fell open in my lap to those double columns of gifts again. *Perception of Spirits*.

My rage turned into an overwhelming feeling of loss and sadness, leaving me bone-tired. It was all I could do to say goodbye to Aimee and, still clutching the book in my hand, stumble to my room.

The sun still wasn't up yet when I dropped gratefully into bed.

Unfortunately, my sleep was far from peaceful.

Chapter 10

The dream hit me before I'd hardly closed my eyes. I was cantering up the long driveway on Bally, just like I had on the day we'd arrived, only this time we were running so slowly as if the air had grown thick and difficult to pass through. Far away I could hear somebody calling my name but I couldn't quite make out the words. I looked down and saw that something looked wrong with the tips of Bally's ears—they'd faded until they were nearly invisible. As I watched, all the colour leached from his grey mane and neck, becoming translucent; I could see the ground rushing by right through him.

"Beware the one who watches," a voice whispered right next to my ear, "the lady rides nine." And then Bally was gone and I was tumbling end over end straight toward the forest floor, still moving slowly as if through water. I hit the ground with barely a thud and lay there, wondering what on earth had happened. Suddenly a figure was standing over me, regarding me sadly through a pair of ice-blue eyes. Her long red hair tumbled over her shoulders. She didn't look as bedraggled as she had last time. There were no leaves in her hair and her dress was clean and untorn.

"Evangeline?" I asked but she didn't answer; just shook her head and pointed toward the woods.

"What?" I said, turning my head to look into the forest. I squinted as something dark flashed between the trees. Was it human or animal? When I turned back to her she was gone and I was all alone.

I woke from the dream with a violent start, sitting bolt upright in the darkness with my heart thundering away in my chest. The curtains were drawn tight and there was no early morning light yet to cut through the inky blackness. I had the sudden, awful feeling that I was not alone. Somebody was with me in my room.

Clutching the covers to my chest, I sat stone-still, holding my breath and listening for all I was worth. Was that a soft footstep on the carpet near the door? A quiet exhalation from beside my bed? Was someone, right now, reaching out to touch me?

Right then, a faint draft of cold air brushed across my cheek and I screamed involuntarily, throwing myself to the side to avoid an imagined assailant. There was a sharp thud of something falling and then the sound of breaking glass. I rolled to the far side of the bed and threw myself to the floor, landing hard on my hip and crying out again. There was a scuttling sound and a door slammed and then another.

The lights flicked on and I screamed again. Suddenly Gil was right there beside me lifting me gently to my feet.

"You're okay, you're okay," he kept repeating, pulling me hard against his chest where his heartbeat lub-lubbed away almost as fast as mine was. "What happened, Jilly?"

"There ... was ... someone ... in here," I gasped, "here in my room. I felt them touch me."

"Okay, calm down. Tell me slowly what happened."

I told him about my nightmare and then of waking up with the utter certainty that I was not alone.

"And you felt someone touch you?"

"I ... I think so. I could hear them breathing, too."

Xan appeared in the bedroom doorway wearing a pair of black and gold silk pajamas along with matching slippers and a silk eye mask pushed up to the top of his head that made him look like a young sultan. He also had a disgruntled-looking Morris under one arm.

"What on earth is all this about, Jilly? It's five o clock in the morning. Some of us need to sleep a full eight hours."

"Shut up, you idiot," Gil snapped. "Can't you see she's terrified? Did you see anyone in the hall as you came in?"

"Just this mangy creature," he said, dropping Morris unceremoniously onto my bed. "He came streaking into my room the second I opened my door. Something spooked him. Probably all the screaming; I was having the loveliest dream, you know."

"I'm sorry you lost your beauty sleep," Gil said dryly. He sat me down on the bed and moved to the dresser where the little figurines had all been knocked over. The front end of a little horse had smashed into a thousand pieces and they lay scattered across the floor. But the back end was completely intact. Gilbert picked it up carefully turning it over and over in both hands. "I remember these," he said, "this is like the ones your mother has at home, the ones you used to hide things in."

"What are you talking about?" I asked incredulously. "I've never seen anything like that before."

"Sure, you have, you showed me that time we were exploring during a rainstorm. There was a hidden compartment inside; you twist the horse in half and it comes apart. It's like a secret chamber.

"Gilbert, I have no idea what you're talking about. We have nothing like that at home. I would definitely remember that."

"Well, we'll just add it to one of the many things you don't remember about our childhood," he said, raising his eyebrows. "You'll just have to trust me on this one."

He fished inside the little compartment and pulled out a small fragment of torn paper.

"What is that?" Xan leaned closer so he could see better, then grabbed the piece of paper, "it's just a drawing of some girl on a horse. Who would bother to hide that?"

"Jilly," Gil said sharply, pointing to a closed door beside the entry for the bathroom, "where does that door go to?"

"I have no idea. I assumed it was a closet."

"I can answer that," Xan said, casting a superior look at Gil. "I have one in my room, too. Most of the rooms here are adjoining. I discovered mine ages ago, but I'm not surprised that an unobservant fellow such as yourself would miss something so obvious."

"Damn it, this place is a maze," Gil said, pulling the door open and peering into the next room, this one decorated in shades of pink. "I don't like this; these people aren't trustworthy at all."

"Don't get excited over nothing," Xan said in a bored voice. "Estelle told me all about it. Technically it was for fire protection, there weren't any windows in half of these rooms so it was another way to escape in an emergency. But she said the real reason is that the man who first built the house, or at least this wing of it, was a horrible letch who needed a secret way to meet his mistresses. She said there are more passageways in the house, too."

"Oh, great," Gil said, looking around the room as if he expected more passageways to spring up before his eyes.

"It *is* a bit creepy," I agreed, wondering why Belinda had left that chunk of history lesson out when I was getting my tour.

"Stay here with Xan," Gil ordered, "I'll be right back."

He slipped through the door into the next room and I felt a spark of unease as he left.

Come on, pull yourself together, I told myself firmly, *stop being such a baby.*

"Look, what's that?" Xan said, coming closer and kneeling beside the broken shards of porcelain. He reached out and carefully nudged aside a few pieces to pick up a tiny object, no bigger than a rolled cigarette. It was the same shape as a cigarette except hollow and tied with a tiny red cord of embroidery thread in the middle.

"That's strange," I said, taking the paper from him carefully. "It looks … it looks like a miniature scroll of some sort. And look, there's a piece torn out of it at one end. Do you think it was part of the paper in the figurine?"

"I don't know." Xan shrugged. "Go on and open it, though, and see what it says."

"I'm not sure…it's not our house—"

"Oh, go on, if it's something important then we'll turn it over to Estelle, of course. If you don't open it, then I will."

"Okay, okay." I pulled delicately at the little string with the tips of my fingers, careful not to damage anything. It came apart easily though, and I unfurled the minuscule piece of paper.

"The lady rides nine," I read. "Sorry, that's all it says."

A shiver went through me as I remembered the lady saying that in my dream. What did it mean though?

"The lady rides nine. Nine what? Horses?" Xan asked.

"I have no idea. Maybe *at* nine o'clock? Your guess is as good as mine."

"Well, if somebody went to the trouble to put it inside the horse sculpture then it must be important."

"You don't think that the person in my room was searching for that, do you?" I gulped and suppressed a shiver.

"I wonder..." Xan said slowly. "Where on earth is that stable boy, anyway?"

"Here," Gil said, sticking his head back inside the door. "This place is like a rabbit warren, nearly all the rooms are connected and none of the doors lock. It's ridiculous."

"All right then, Sherlock," Xan said, "Did you manage to catch whoever was in Jilly's room then?"

"No." Gil shrugged reluctantly. "I didn't see a soul."

He turned and marched back in the direction he'd come from.

"Maybe we're making more out of this than we need to," Xan said quietly as soon as Gil was out of earshot."

"All right, so who was in my room then? I didn't make it up."

"Morris, of course. He was prowling around, knocked over the horses, scared himself and bolted into the hall."

"But what touched my face?"

"Wind from the corridor? It's pretty drafty here."

"Hmm," I said doubtfully, "maybe." But I couldn't shake off the absolute certainty that someone had been here.

"From now on we stick together," Gil said, appearing again in the room next to mine. He deposited his luggage on the bed with a thump. "You should probably take the room beside me, Xan, that way we can keep an eye on each other."

"No thank you, my room is quite comfortable. If you two want to canoodle down here in your love nest, by all means, be my guest."

"Get out," Gil said fiercely, pointing toward the door.

"Gladly, I have some sleep to catch up on. Have a good time, you two." Xan sashayed from the room, throwing a meaningful glance over his shoulder.

"Gah, how do you stand him?" Gil said, thrusting his hands in his pockets.

"Oh, he grows on you."

"Like a bad mold," Gil said morosely.

"Yes, a little like that. But he does care in his own way. Thank you for coming to rescue me. I guess, now that I think about it, it *could* have been Morris that scared me as Xan said. I woke up from that awful nightmare and … well, I guess my mind could have been playing tricks on me. I'm a little distracted right now."

"Hmm," Gil said. "Well, I think I trust your judgement better than Xan's; if you say there was someone in here, then there was. Anyway, let's see if we can get a bit more sleep before the sun comes up. We have a big day of riding ahead. I'll be right here next door if you need me. We'll leave the doors open between our rooms."

It took me a long time to go back to sleep, even with Gil snoring away in the room next to mine. I couldn't help but wish that he'd just stayed with me. It was so much easier to breathe when he was right beside me. But, despite my troubled thoughts, I finally managed to drift off.

I didn't wake up until the sun was high overhead and Aimee was pushing my breakfast trolley noisily across the floor. And it wasn't until I was on my second cup of coffee that I realized something important; the book I'd set on my bedside table, the one my great, great grandfather had written, had disappeared.

Chapter 11

When I shared the news on the way to the barn after breakfast, neither Xan nor Gil knew what to make of it. They hadn't seen me with the book in the first place, so they weren't much help in looking for it.

"But why would anyone steal some old book from you now?" Xan asked. "If it's been kept in the library this whole time then anyone living here could have read it any time they wanted."

"Hmm, good point," I said, "it doesn't make any sense."

"Unless someone just didn't want Jilly to read it," Gil said darkly.

We were almost to the front door when Belinda waylaid me. "Jillian, could I have a word, please?"

"Umm." All I wanted to do was go to the barn and see Bally but I didn't want to seem rude. A few minutes wouldn't hurt.

"Sure, okay," I said, trying not to sound *too* encouraging. "I have to help in the barn soon, but I can spare a few minutes."

"Perfect." Her eyes lit up and she clasped her hands

together. "I'll meet you in the library then. I just have to finish up a few things in the kitchen and then I'll be right there."

Fine, I thought with a sigh and resigned myself to another uncomfortable conversation.

"We'll wait with you," Gil said, looking meaningfully at Xan.

"Afraid you're on your own." Xan pulled on his riding gloves and sauntered toward the door where Estelle was waiting.

"Good morning," Estelle called to us but she didn't look like she'd had a very solid night's sleep either. Her face was pale and the dark circles under her eyes gave her a gaunt, hunted look.

"Gil, you go ahead with them. I'll be fine. I'll be out in a few minutes once I've talked to Belinda." I still hadn't come to terms with all these new revelations; I wasn't even sure if I completely believed everything. I certainly wasn't ready to talk about it with Gil hovering over me protectively. His suspicions had only deepened overnight and he was unusually surly this morning.

He protested a little and then finally gave in. "Fine, you have half an hour and then I come looking for you."

I waited for them all to leave and then went a few steps down the hallway to the small, library door. Just as I put my hand on the latch, I heard the sound of glass breaking and a startled cry from inside.

"Aimee?" I said, pushing the door open. She knelt on the carpet on the far side of the room, sweeping up the remains of a porcelain figurine that had shattered when it fell. "Are you hurt?"

Aimee's face flushed a deep shade of red, and she brushed hurriedly at her eyes. "Oh, I'm just clumsy this morning," she said in frustration. "This is one of Ruthie's favourite figurines; she'll be so upset when she finds out I've broken it."

"Here, let me help." I reached out but she batted my hand away impatiently, her fingernails scraping across my arm.

I looked down at the shallow scratches in surprise.

"Sorry, sorry," she said hastily, "I didn't mean to do that, you just startled me. Stand back now. I don't want you to get cut on any of these shards."

She had to brush past me to reach the garbage can, and I could see that her hands were shaking badly. She dumped the broken sculpture in the bin but instead of leaving it at that she lifted the garbage can and clutched it in her arms, backing out the doorway into the hall with a strange look on her face.

Well, what on earth was all that about? I thought, watching her go in astonishment. *She looked like she'd seen a ghost.*

That wasn't my only surprise, though; when I glanced down at the little table I'd been seated next to earlier that morning, I saw that the little black book had returned.

Well, how bizarre, I thought, going over to pick it up. It was unharmed, and I still got that distasteful, shivery feeling when I touched the cover, almost as if it were alive. I set it down again abruptly, wiping my hands on my breeches.

My gaze travelled to the large display case that dominated the wall in the far corner, where Aimee had been kneeling.

"I wonder what Aimee was doing when she broke that sculpture?" I murmured to myself quietly. "She didn't have a duster with her so she couldn't have been cleaning. And she certainly didn't want me to see those broken shards of pottery. Was there something hidden in that statue, too? Was it another silly riddle on a scroll? Gil's right, there is something strange going on here."

I was pulled from my thoughts by a soft scratching sound and I looked down to see Morris busily sharpening his oversized claws on the door jamb, leaving small scratch marks in the wood.

"No, no," I said quickly, scooping him up into my arms.

"We're not in a barn, Morris, if you want to be a house cat then you can't just claw anywhere you feel like."

He bunted his head against my chin, breaking into a happy rumbling purr, and my heart melted. Just as suddenly he stiffened, lifted his head, and stared at the doorway, unblinking like an owl.

"What is it, Morris?" I asked just as a floorboard creaked loudly in the hallway nearby. "Don't worry, it's just Belinda coming back."

But Aimee had left the door wide open when she had scuttled away and I could see now that the hallway was empty.

"Old houses always make strange noises," I told the cat, hugging him closer to my chest

But still, I jumped when the floor creaked loudly again, this time closer.

"Hello?" I called instinctively, holding my breath as I waited for a response.

Of course, there was no answer and after a moment I relaxed. It was just the floors settling in this creepy old house. They did that back home at Greystone sometimes when the weather changed.

Morris let out a loud yowling sound that nearly scared me out of my skin. He twisted in my arms and hit the ground with a thud, all his fur rising on end as he stared at something outside the library.

He puffed up like a Halloween cat and moved sideways into the hall, his tail lashing stiffly.

Meeeeeoowwww, he said in a low warning voice.

"Morris? What on earth has gotten into you? There's nothing there."

Moving faster than I'd ever seen him run, he shot down the hallway toward the stairs. He turned back once to look at me with wide, yellow eyes, and then put a large paw on the staircase.

"Morris, no," I hissed, hurrying down the hall toward him. "We can't go up there, you have to stay downstairs."

He paused for a moment to listen and then, like all members of his species, he ignored me completely and did exactly the opposite of what I wanted. By the time I got there, he was already up the stairs and on the landing, standing on his hind legs with his front paws resting against the stained-glass portrait of the Dark Lady.

"Oh my gosh, Morris, no. Get down here."

He didn't even look back; he was so intent on peering into the glass that he didn't hear me at all.

Aimee had already said in no uncertain terms that this part of the house was off-limits, but I knew I needed to get Morris down from there before he started exploring any further. If I could catch him then I could distract him with his breakfast and he'd probably forget all about adventuring.

I crept up the stairs to the landing, pausing to glance at the magnificent window up close. I could see now why people paid money to come and tour this place. The details in the glass were exquisite. I reached out my hand and lightly brushed it against the copper shoulder of the horse but the second I did a cold gust of air blasted down the hall toward me, tugging my hair, and running up and down my arms with icy fingers. I leapt back in surprise, wrapping my arms around myself to stave off the cold.

As soon as the wind ruffled his fur, Morris let out another high-pitched otherworldly yowl and his orange, tabby coat puffed out until he was four times his size. He flattened his ears against his head and bolted the rest of the way up the stairs, disappearing into the dimly lit hallway above.

There was a low, scrabbling sound behind me, like claws click-clacking across the floor or a beetle scuttling, making my hair stand on end. I spun around but the foyer was empty, just the steady ticking of the grandfather clock behind me broke the silence. Suddenly, I didn't want to be there anymore, not on this stairway and not in this house. I wanted to race to the barn and find Gil, throw Bally in the trailer and drive away from this place as fast as I could.

"Morris," I hissed. "Come back here, you coward." But there was no sign of him.

The icy wind disappeared just as quickly as it had arrived and I looked suspiciously at the stained glass but didn't risk touching it again.

Taking a deep breath, I climbed the last few steps to the upper floor, walking softly on the thick carpet. With any luck, I could find Morris and escape back downstairs without anyone catching me up here.

The short hallway was lined with tightly closed doors and there was no sign of the cat and yet also nowhere that I could see for him to hide. I crept down the hall, too afraid to test any of the doorknobs in case someone was behind one of them.

Nothing, I sighed as I reached the last closed door. *Where could he have gone?* I'd have to turn around and try the opposite corridor even though I was sure I'd seen him bolt this way.

I paused as a low scrabbling, scratching noise sounded just behind the last door. Was that Morris clawing again? Or was it something more sinister?

Holding my breath, I reached out to touch the heavy wooden door, turning the knob ever so slowly. The scratching stopped, and then there was a sharp cry and the sound of breaking glass. I thought I could make out a faint cry for help.

"Hello," I called, wrenching at the doorknob but it was stuck fast. "Are you okay? Do you need help?"

I tried the door again just to be certain it was locked and then scanned up and down the hall to see if there might be another way in. *Maybe there's a secret passage to get in*, I thought, *Xan said something about that in all the drama this morning.*

I searched the hallway, running my hands along the walls

but try as I might I could not find any sign of hidden doorways or secret passages.

Another cold breeze passed over me and I shuddered involuntarily, rubbing my arms to get rid of the chill. There was a low scraping noise behind me like that of a key turning in a lock followed by the creaking of hinges. I spun around just in time to see the door swing open of its own accord.

I froze, my heart beating wildly in my chest and my hair standing on end. What in the world was going on here?

I was so scared that I let out a little scream when Morris trotted out of the room and rubbed up against my legs as if he hadn't a care in the world.

What on earth? I held my breath and forced myself toward the doorway, even though every nerve in my body was urging me to run hard in the opposite direction. The room was utterly dark. I reached in and ran my hand tentatively up the wall on the inside of the door, sighing with relief when my fingers found a light switch.

Here goes nothing, I thought, flipping the switch upward.

Soft ambient light flooded the room, revealing a canopy bed covered in silver brocade at least three times the size of my bed in the guest room. The chamber was nicely decorated with wooden desks, dressers, bookshelves, and sea-chests everywhere. Thick curtains covered the wide double windows so that no light seeped through.

I froze again in the doorway, my hand over my mouth. There in the middle of the gigantic bed, lying still as death with her eyes open, was Great Aunt Ruth.

Chapter 12

I stood frozen, turned to stone for what felt like an eternity before finally, my blood started pumping again and I sprang into action.

"Aunt Ruth," I cried rushing to her bedside. As I drew close, I saw her take one long, unsteady breath. Her eyes flickered and her gaze drifted toward me. She was alive, but barely.

"Aunt Ruth?" I said uncertainly. "It's Jillian, can you hear me?"

Her mouth worked up and down a few times as she struggled to speak. I leaned as close as I dared to try to catch her hoarse whisper.

"The lady," she wheezed. "The lady rides nine."

Ugh, the Lady again. Why was it always about that damned lady?

"Forget her. Are you hurt? Do you need help?"

"Look to the lady," she said, breathing raggedly. "The lady rides nine."

That's what the scroll said, I thought, my mind whirling. *It must be important. Either way, I have to help her get out of here. We need the police and a hospital. I can't believe she's been kept prisoner here all this time. I can't believe Aimee, Estelle and Belinda would lie like this. Were they all in on it?*

I looked down at her frail body and knew that she was in no position to move. I had to go find Gil and Xan and get us out of here. I hated to leave her like this, though.

"Hang on just a little longer, Aunt Ruth," I told her. "I'm going to go get help."

"Wait," she said clutching my sleeve. "The lady rides nine."

"Okay, yes, that's nice," I told her patting her sleeve, "but I need to help you now. We need to go to the hospital."

I turned toward the doorway reluctantly, not wanting to leave her all by herself. Someone here in the house, maybe *everyone* here, wanted her harmed. And I had no idea whom I could trust.

"Stay here," I said, although clearly, she wasn't going anywhere.

I took one step toward the door and then heard a heavy tread out on the landing. I looked around the room in a panic, hoping to find a quick place to hide, but by then it was too late.

The door flew open in one swift move and Belinda framed the doorway, holding a tray.

"Jillian," she said in bewilderment. "How on earth did you get in here? I thought we were going to meet in the library."

Well, that answers my question about Belinda, I thought sadly. I'd just been beginning to like her. Her sister Betty would be so disappointed.

Belinda stared at me quizzically and then set the tray carefully down on the dresser beside the door.

"Now, now, child," she said coaxingly, looking into my face. "I can see you're upset but it's not what you think at all. Why don't you sit down and I'll explain everything?"

"I don't think so," I said defensively, backing away from her and eyeing up the open door. If only I could get her to come further into the room, maybe I could make a break for it and reach the door before she could. "You lied to us about Ruth being away in France or Florida or whatever you made up, and you're keeping her captive here. I've seen how movies like this end; you're going to try and lock me up and kill me, too, because I know too much. You won't get away with this; lots of people know where we are."

"Oh, for Heaven's sake," Belinda said in exasperation. "Why are young people always so dramatic? Nobody's killing anybody, Jillian. Now if you'll just listen, I'll explain everything."

"I think you can tell the police your explanation. I don't want to hear it."

"Oh, my dear, I'm afraid that won't do at all," she said, her smile dropping away. She moved closer and I shrank backward with an involuntary cry.

But instead of attacking, she reached out for a velvet cord that hung from a hook just inside the door. She pulled hard on it three times and I heard a bell chime deep within the house.

"Now we wait," she said, standing with her body blocking the door. She stared at me curiously. "How on earth did you get in here, though? I'm sure the door was locked."

"I don't know," I snapped, not in the mood to answer any of her questions. "I only came upstairs to catch Morris, but he disappeared. And when I came to this doorway, I could hear him inside and there was the sound of breaking glass and someone screamed."

"Was there?" Belinda said sharply, peering around the room. I turned to look over my shoulder, too, wondering what I'd heard. Aunt Ruth didn't look in the position to have been up out of bed breaking things. Had someone else been in here? Was there another way to get out of the room?

"Yes," I said slowly, "the door wouldn't open at first and then it just popped open on its own. I don't understand it, either, honestly."

Belinda looked at me thoughtfully. "It's probably The Lady. She's attached to Ruth, you see."

"Okay, that's enough," I snapped, my nerves on edge. "I don't have time for more lies."

She opened her mouth to answer but then turned at the sound of feet stomping up the stairs.

I shrank back even further, bracing myself for the worst. Where, oh where, was Gil now that I truly needed him? Surely a half an hour had passed by now.

Jacob pushed into the doorway, holding his cane between his hands like a baseball bat and I was reminded of my dream when that very cane was used to bludgeon Great Aunt Ruth to death.

"I knew it," he growled, "I knew she was trouble the first time I laid eyes on her. I should have finished her off while I had the chance."

"Now, now," Belinda said sharply, "that's enough of that. There won't be any more violence in this house. Let's go downstairs and talk it over properly like we should have done in the first place."

"All of you are in on it?" I said, fueled by a mixture of anger and sadness. "You all hated Ruth enough to kidnap her?"

"No, of course not, dear," Belinda said, "Ruthie is like a sister to me, none of us would ever hurt her. We're just trying to protect her. All will be explained."

I scooped up Morris from where he was lying next to Ruth and took one last look at her pale face, hoping that I could figure out a way to help her, and myself, out of this mess.

"Go ahead," Jacob said roughly, giving me a little push toward the hall.

With every trembling step I took, I half expected to be shoved down the staircase or bludgeoned with Jacob's cane. I heaved a breath of relief when I made it safely to the bottom.

They shut me and Morris into one of the small, windowless sitting rooms without another word. As soon as the door locked behind me, I sank into one of the chairs by the fire and buried my face in Morris's fur, shaky with adrenaline.

I don't know how long I sat there but finally, there was a noise by the door and Morris twisted himself out of my grasp and leapt nimbly to the ground.

I looked up to see Estelle leaning on her crutches in the doorway, a pained expression on her face.

"Oh Jilly," she said earnestly, "I'm so sorry you found out this way. Now you must think we're all heartless monsters but, honestly, everything we did was to help Ruth, not to hurt her."

I narrowed my eyes in her direction, not saying a word. There was nothing she could say at this point that would make me trust her again. If, no *when*, I got out of here I would go to the police and make sure that every one of them spent a long time in jail.

"You don't believe me, I know. But I'll tell you everything once everyone gets here. I promise."

We sat for ages in uncomfortable, miserable silence until Gil and Xan pushed into the room, cheeks still flushed from riding.

Belinda followed closely behind, and she and Jacob stood blocking the doorway, a barrier to keep us from escaping.

"Jillian, what's wrong? What's going on?" Gil asked, his gaze zeroing in on the wretched expression on my face.

I hadn't allowed myself to feel too much panic up until now, but the sight of him made me weak with relief and tears sprang to my eyes.

"I have no idea," I said bitterly. "Great Aunt Ruth isn't on vacation at all. She's here and she's alive, but barely. They've been hiding her upstairs all this time."

"I knew it," Gil swore and strode to my side, sitting down beside me and holding my hand tightly. "Are you hurt?"

"No, but I want to go home," I said.

"We won't keep you against your will and I can assure you we didn't kidnap Ruth," Estelle said earnestly, her eyes fixed on Xan. "We love her and we only want what's best for her."

"That's certainly not what it looked like," I said.

"I know, and I'm sorry you had to see her that way. Ruth has been sick off and on since spring. She's been seeing her doctor regularly and doing tests at the hospital, but they can't figure out what's wrong. She didn't want to tell anyone; she wanted to keep it a secret. She thought that if her family knew that she was failing that they'd descend on her like locusts, trying to get their hands on her money. She just assumed she'd get better ... but she hasn't."

"But if she's that sick then she should be in the hospital," Xan said quietly, disappointment stamped across his features.

"Oh, but she'd hate that. Doctor Crane is an old family friend and he comes every few days to check on her. She's had the best of care. But she's old and weak; there's only so much the doctor can do to keep her alive. It was her wish to stay in her own home and the doctor respects that. Ruthie is much better off staying here with us."

"Fine," Gil said, "let's take your word on that part for now. But why keep it a secret from us? Why lock her in her room?"

"Because, before she became very ill, she warned us that we were to do our utmost to protect the estate from her relatives. It wasn't that we didn't trust you specifically, but we'd promised her to keep her secret."

"Estelle," Aimee hissed sharply from the doorway. She pushed past Belinda and Jacob and stood in the middle of the room, her hair undone and standing up wildly in all directions "Stop talking, you're ruining everything."

"No, I'm not," Estelle insisted. "Jill discovered Ruth on her own so there's no point in keeping secrets anymore. I trust them and I think they can help."

"It doesn't matter what you think. It's not your secret to share. We can find it on our own."

"Now, now," Belinda said, "I agree with Estelle. We haven't been able to find it so far, have we? And we're running out of time. Maybe they can help."

"You're all talking in circles," Xan said. "What are we supposed to be finding?"

"Ruth's will," Estelle said with a sigh. "She'd given us strict instructions to take it to her lawyer if she ever fell too ill. But when I went to find it, it was gone."

"Can't you just ask her where it is, though? She spoke to me upstairs."

"Did she?" Estelle asked in surprise. "Are you sure? She hasn't said anything to us for days. She's in some sort of semi-lucid state that she won't fully wake up from. The doctor honestly has no idea what's wrong. She can eat, she can blink, and we think she can understand a few things, but she's not in her right mind at all. We owe it to her to find the will. Otherwise, the estate will revert to her awful family. No offence."

"But how do you even know that there's a will at all?" I asked.

There was a long silence while everyone in the room exchanged glances.

"Well," Estelle said slowly, "because the night that she first fell into this state, all she could talk about was her will.

"There was a terrific storm that raged all day and night and the power kept flickering off and on. Ruth was frantic that she wouldn't get the will finished. She was up all night revising and rewriting it. It was like she was possessed and couldn't stop. She kept us up, too, what with her prowling around the house and calling us every time she had a new version for us to witness. It was awful. I don't even know how many of them she made.

"What do you mean by *them*?" Xan asked. "There can only be one final will."

"Who are you to say how many wills a person can have?" Jacob snapped, glaring at Xan. "You city folk think you can come in here and—"

"That's enough, Jacob," Belinda interrupted gently. "As Estelle was saying, the night Ruthie wrote her will she was so agitated. That storm didn't help her nerves. She felt … well, she felt that someone was watching her and maybe even trying to influence her. I was horrible to see her like that."

"Who was watching her?" Gil asked, frowning.

"She never said but I don't think … I don't think it was a real person. Over the last few months, she'd begun to act strangely. You know she sent away all the staff; first the housekeepers, and then the gardeners and finally, the stable help. She'd become paranoid. She thought someone was watching her. Something, well, evil."

We all fell into silent contemplation.

"Anyway," Estelle went on, "Ruth spent all night in her office writing and writing. She wouldn't let any of us go to bed. She just kept ringing the bell every hour or so and calling us in two at a time to witness each will. But she didn't share the contents with any of us. We're not sure if it's the same will or if she changed her mind over and over again. There could be one will or there could be five or even ten. We're not sure. At this point, we'd be glad to find just one of them."

"What do you mean? Where did they go?" Xan asked.

"We have no idea," Estelle said. "I came into the office that morning and found her slumped over her desk. There was a pen in her hand, but the wills were nowhere to be found."

"So, you have no idea who will inherit the estate then?" Xan said.

"No, I guess we don't," Estelle said, sending him a sharp look. "Ruth had talked at one point about leaving the whole estate to charity, so it's quite possible that's what she did. She definitely didn't want to leave it to her family, although she did speak highly of *you*, Xan. I think she secretly wanted you to come help us train the horses since I'm such a washout at jumping. So, if any family members were to inherit, it would be you."

"Well, I wouldn't turn free money away," Xan said, "but, I never put much faith in inheriting anything. I wouldn't have minded if she'd wanted to be my sponsor, though. I've always wanted a sponsor."

"Of course, our greatest wish is to have the estate stay as it is," Estelle said firmly. "It would be awful to see the horses sold and all of Ruthie's hard work turn to nothing. And I would miss this place terribly."

"As would we all," Belinda agreed, wiping a stray tear off her cheek. "This has been my home for over forty years. I don't know what I'll do when it's gone."

"And poor Jacob has lost the most," Estelle added sympathetically, looking toward the door where Jacob still stood guard.

"None of that, it's not over yet," he said roughly, gripping his cane with both hands. "You're all talking about her as if she's already dead; she still might rally."

"Of course, she might," Estelle assured him hastily.

"Why, Jacob?" I asked bluntly. It wasn't the politest of questions, but I was pretty sure the fact that they'd kidnapped my aunt was enough to cancel out social niceties.

"Well," Estelle said slowly, "Ruth didn't want to tell anyone until after the wedding because she thought her family would cause some sort of trouble if they knew. But before she became ill, Jacob and Ruth were engaged to be married."

"*Married*," I said in astonishment and was rewarded by another spiteful glare from Jacob.

"Don't sound so uppity about it," he snapped, "we would

have married years ago when we were just young things in love, but her parents forbid the match and sent her away. We didn't see each other for years but when we met again, it was just like no time had ever passed. When she finally returned here to live, after her parent's death, Ruth hired me on as a groundskeeper. I'm not sure that it fooled anyone but it was the only way we could be together."

"So, what changed?" I asked. "Why get married now?"

"Age came with wisdom, I suppose. We both figured that we deserved to enjoy the last few years we had to spend here on earth. And that's a lesson to you young folk … don't fritter away your best days like we did. When you figure out what you want out of life, you don't let anything stand in your way."

My eyes prickled at the emotion in his voice and I involuntarily glanced toward Gil who still had me tucked protectively at my side.

"We were going to travel the world together, see all the sights we missed out on the first time," Jacob said, his voice rough with emotion.

"That's why Ruthie was so obsessed with the legend of the Dark Lady," Belinda said softly. "Evangeline and Phillippe were star-crossed lovers, too. Her grandfather, Alocious, was a miserly man who had a cruel streak, just like Evangeline's father. Those books he wrote were not nearly as hateful as the person he was in real life, and he passed many of those traits down to his son, Ruth's father."

"So let me get this straight," Gil said, getting back to the point. "Ruth had begun to worry about her health and decided that she and Jacob would get married. Then she gets sicker and starts becoming paranoid that she's being watched and fires almost everyone who works on the estate. Then a few nights before the wedding, she writes a bunch of wills and has various combinations of everyone here witness them. And then that night, she falls into the strange state and never regains her mind again."

"Yes," Estelle said slowly, "that's about it, I suppose."

"And did you look for the wills?"

"Of course, we did," Aimee said indignantly, "we've searched the whole house from top to bottom."

"So, either someone took them or she hid them," Gil said.

"Well, nobody here would have *taken* them," Estelle said. "We think that she'd become so paranoid that she hid them somewhere. The thing is that we owe it to her to find the will, or wills, before anyone else in her family discovers how sick she is. That's why we wanted to keep you away. Without a will, the estate will be broken up, and the money will just go to her awful brothers and sisters. There's no way she would have wanted that."

Well, that part is the truth, I thought. My own grandmother Rosalie had been a tyrant and from what I remembered, the rest of those siblings were no better. *Maybe Great Aunt Ruth was the nice one of the group.* I had very few memories of my grandmother other than generally being afraid of her, but I did remember her sharp tongue and scathing remarks had made my mother seem like a lamb in comparison.

"And of course, that's when we arrived and ruined your plans," Xan said angrily.

"Will you stay and help us?" Estelle asked, staring intently at Xan. "You know our secret now. If everyone helps to search the house then we might have a chance of finding the will before it's too late."

"I don't see why we should," Xan said, his face flushing. "You lied to us from the beginning and you locked up a defenseless old woman. I think we need to get Ruth to the hospital today and then leave you all for the police to deal with."

"We could help you before we leave on two conditions," Gil

interrupted, ignoring the outraged glare Xan sent him. "You get the doctor back here today to check on Ruth and make sure she doesn't need to be in a hospital tonight."

"But we've already told you—" Estelle began.

"And secondly, you explain why Jilly has a lump on her head the size of an orange. Because there's no way she ever fell off that horse; she was attacked."

There was dead silence, and if the situation hadn't been so serious, I would have laughed at the guilty expressions on everyone's faces.

"Er, well, about that," Estelle said, blushing crimson.

"You see, it was more of an *accident* than an attack," Belinda said, twisting her apron between both hands. "Estelle took off galloping on that fool horse of hers and when she didn't return, we grew frightened. Ruthie took a sudden turn for the worse, nearly at the moment when Estelle left the house. She started tossing and turning in her bed and muttering all sorts of things about the Lady and Estelle. We didn't know what to do."

"And then you come barging up to the house, banging on the door and making all that racket," Jacob growled, lowering his eyebrows at me menacingly. "How were we supposed to know what was happening? All I could think of was my promise to my sweet Ruthie that I wouldn't let her meddling relatives barge their way into our lives. And, well, I might have acted a little hastily; I'll confess that much, and I might have hit you a little harder than I'd intended. I meant to just give you a light *tap*, see, to just put you gently to sleep so we could ship you back where you came from. But, I suppose I put a little too much strength behind it. I had no idea I still had it in me."

He faltered into silence then glanced at me, wiping his hand nervously across his brow. "And, well, I guess I'm sorry. You don't seem like a bad sort after all."

"You could have killed her," Gil said tightly, "and I swear

that if any of you so much as touch a single hair on Jilly's head again that you will regret the moment you were ever born. Is that understood?"

They all nodded solemnly and I felt Gil's grip on my hand loosen a little. "Good, now who is going to call this doctor in to see Ruthie?"

Chapter 13

The rest of that tense and awkward day passed slowly, although I don't think anyone got through it very comfortably. The doctor had been called and was scheduled to come that evening so we somehow had to go about our business, though we were all still shocked after the morning's events.

Xan and Gil came with me to see Great Aunt Ruth, who looked the same as when I'd left her earlier. She didn't say anything this time, though, just flicked her eyes open and gave Xan a little smile before falling back asleep.

Gil, Xan, and I went down to the barn with Estelle limping behind us to work with the horses, but despite Estelle's anxious attempts to make small-talk, that easy camaraderie from the last few days had disappeared.

Xan was uncharacteristically silent and he kept sending Estelle angry, lingering glances that made her blush and look away. She'd tried to corner him in the feed room to apologize for lying, but he'd just brushed her away and went on with his work.

He must have really liked her if his feelings are that hurt, I thought, *poor Xan never gives his heart to anyone.*

We did our chores mainly in silence, turning the non-working horses out one by one and tidying their stalls while Estelle sat alone in the tack room cleaning the saddles and bridles.

Gil hovered protectively near me while we worked, but my morning had been so disturbing that I didn't mind it nearly so much as I normally would. I got Bally brushed and tacked up in record time, and then handed him over to Gil to ride.

Xan was already onboard Rigel when we came in and the big horse seemed to be in a perfectly good mood, trotting happily around the far end of the ring.

Muted sunlight drifted in through the windows overhead, casting flickering shadows across the arena.

Something caught my eye and I jerked my head up, looking past where Xan and Rigel were training.

For a second, I could have sworn that I saw that same tall, thin man who'd been lurking in the woods earlier. He stood in the corner, his gaze narrowed directly at me. But of course, it was just a trick of the light; I blinked and there was nothing there at all.

Gil swung up on Bally and was looking down adjusting his feet in the stirrups when the explosion happened.

With an enraged squeal, Rigel spooked sideways in the far corner, twisting in the air. Then he took off in a series of violent bucks that must have rattled every bone in Xan's body. He leapt and plunged like a fish caught on a hook, desperately shaking his head from side to side trying to get away. It was a rodeo-worthy performance that would have launched a less-determined rider into the wall.

Xan hung on grimly, but it was like trying to ride on top of a twisting and turning roller coaster that also wanted to kill you.

Gil had pulled an astonished-looking Bally off to one corner of the ring to keep him out of harm's way and was watching Xan with a serious expression on his face. I could see him debating if he needed to step in and help somehow when Rigel stopped his shenanigans as abruptly as he'd started. His flattened ears pricked forward and he began to trot obediently around the ring like a well-trained school pony.

"Good grief," Xan said shakily, drawing Rigel to a halt, "what on earth was that?"

'Wow, Xan, are you okay?" I asked. "I can't believe you stayed on through all that. Well done."

"I think I need a stiff drink after that. I don't know what set him off, though."

"There was that weird shadow in the corner," I said, frowning in that direction. "It must have frightened him."

"He didn't look scared exactly." Gil started circling Bally around the ring on a loose rein to stretch out his muscles. "He seemed angry."

"Well, he knows who his master is now," Xan said, shooting a glance over to where Estelle had appeared at the edge of the ring, probably drawn by all the noise. Her face was white and she gripped the top rail with both hands. "He won't pull another stunt like that again."

Gil and I exchanged a look but said nothing. Rigel's unnatural transformation from bucking bronco to docile pony wasn't something I'd ever seen before. He'd acted like he was possessed earlier. I knew one thing; I wouldn't trust or let my guard down around that horse for a single second. There was something not quite right about him.

As soon as Gil and Bally were trotting happily around the ring, I left them to work on their own and went to visit my little friend Damascus, who I'd kept inside so I could brush him.

"Hey, buddy," I said, slipping into his stall and running a hand down his soft, fuzzy shoulder. All the horses back at Greystone had their hair clipped short since Mother liked even the non-working broodmares to look show-ready at every moment. So I didn't often get to see horses in their natural winter coats. Damascus was extra fuzzy, too, like a little teddy bear and I couldn't resist hugging his plush neck.

He ate his hay quietly while I fussed over him, currying his coat until it shone, and carefully brushing out his wispy mane and tail. I picked out his feet and then stood back to admire him. He was growing on me fast; I hadn't liked a horse this much since I'd first laid eyes on Bally. I rarely let myself get attached to any of the sale horses back at Greystone because they were all liable to be sold out from under me just as soon as they started showing potential in the show ring.

Mother didn't have a sentimental bone in her body and wouldn't turn down *any* buyer as long as their wallet was big enough. I never had any say in the matter, either. It would be nice, just for once, to be able to make sure that my projects were placed in the homes that were the best for them rather than just with any random stranger who had money.

That's what Gil and I always talked about, I thought idly, reaching over to scratch Damascus on the withers. *We always said that we had our barn together we'd only pick the kindest, most caring buyers for our horses, people who could give the animals a home for life, not just for a few years.*

I stopped short and frowned. Where had that memory come from?

I rubbed a hand across my head where a sudden headache had begun to throb without warning, pounding away somewhere behind my left temple. The pulsing was so strong that that's all I could hear. Closing my eyes, I leaned back against the stone wall and slid down until I was sitting in the deep straw with my head in my hands.

There wasn't any welcoming darkness behind my eyelids, though; instead, a series of bright pictures flashed relentlessly in front of my eyes. Gil and I as children walking hand in hand through a summer pasture full of grazing broodmares, us running through the house exploring while the rain beat down on the windows. The two of us sitting at the kitchen table with a sea of open notebooks spread out around us while Nanny looked on encouragingly. Me, now a teenager, running through the rainy darkness barefoot with those same notebooks clasped in my arms, alone and desperately afraid.

My eyes shot open and I inhaled a deep, ragged breath, my heart hammering hard in my chest.

I didn't know how long I sat there, but eventually, I was aware of the lumpy stone wall poking into my back and then, at the same moment, I felt warm breath and soft, velvety whiskers brushing across my cheek.

Damascus stood with his nose next to my forehead his eyes half-closed as if he were nearly asleep. I went to push myself upright to pet him but as I moved, a chunk of the stone wall at my back shifted and a bit of the crumbling rock gave way.

Damascus opened his eyes with a startled grunt at the noise and I twisted sideways, kneeling in the straw to repair the damage I'd done.

"This place is falling apart, isn't it, buddy?" I told the little colt as I pushed the stone back into place and clambered to my feet. "Wouldn't you like to come live in the lap of luxury with me and Bally instead?"

Damascus snorted and bobbed his head up and down a few times as if he'd understood and I laughed, scratching him behind the ear.

There was the sound of clopping hooves behind us and Gil appeared, leading a tired and happy Bally behind him.

"I wondered where you were," Gil said, frowning in my direction.

"I'm fine, I was just playing with Damascus. How was Bally?"

"Perfect, as always. I'll clean him up and turn him out. Estelle said he can go out with some of the quieter broodmares."

"Sure, actually, I'll put Damascus out with him too and see how they get along."

Gil shot me a knowing look but said nothing as he led Bally to the wash stall to give him a bath.

The crisp fall air put a bounce in the horse's steps and as soon as we let them go, both Bally and Damascus took off cavorting across the pasture together. The older broodmares were only concerned with eating as much of the last grass of the season as possible so they barely even looked up at the two boys who'd invaded their field.

After that, I helped Gil brush and tack up the rest of the horses he planned to ride.

Xan stayed quiet and withdrawn after his ride on Rigel. He moved slowly while he washed and put away the big horse and, by the time he'd come back from turning Rigel out on pasture, he'd developed a noticeable limp on one side.

"Oh, you're hurt," Estelle said worriedly when she came out of the tack room. "Please don't worry about riding anymore horses; there won't be any point to keeping them fit anyway if Ruth doesn't wake up."

Xan hesitated when Estelle laid an imploring hand on his arm and I could see his resolve to be angry with her wavering.

"Let me get you lunch and an aspirin and you can relax for a while by the fire."

Finally, he gave in.

So much for sticking together, I thought as the two of them disappeared toward the house, leaving me and Gil behind. Still, it gave me a chance to fill Gil in on some of the things I'd missed telling him early that morning; Aimee's mysterious houseguest from early that morning and the tiny scroll inside the sculpture. I didn't tell him about the Perception of Spirits thing yet though. I wasn't quite ready for that.

"What do you think 'The Lady rides nine' thing means?" I said, running a soft brush across the shoulder of an oversized bay mare named Agnes. She was sensitive, and her skin twitched in irritation no matter how carefully I brushed her.

Gil shrugged. "It could mean nine horses, or nine o'clock, or even the number of a train or bus or something."

"Oh, right, I didn't think of buses or trains. It could be the number of steps between one thing or another, like from the stained-glass window to the hall or something else important."

"If we were in one of those old mystery movies we used to like to watch, then it would have something to do with when the light from the full moon shining through the window hits a certain spot on the floor."

"Or maybe at nine o'clock in the morning the light hits a certain spot."

"I suppose we could check that out tomorrow morning if we're still around. It wouldn't hurt to just look."

Despite the seriousness of Great Aunt Ruth's condition, I felt a flicker of excitement ripple through me. I hadn't been this interested in anything but horses for ages. I'd forgotten how Gil and I had used to be obsessed with mysteries and puzzles when we were young. I could feel old, long-dormant ideas begin to rise inside of me; something in my mind seemed to wake and stir in the darkness.

"There's that big grandfather clock in the hallway, too," Gil added thoughtfully, "we could check in there. Maybe it does mean nine o'clock."

Now I just wanted to finish the rest of the horses as quickly as possible so we could go explore the rest of the house.

Gil gave each of his horses a careful workout while I busied myself tacking them up and cooling them down in turn so he could just focus on riding. Working as a team we managed to have them all done in under two hours.

"Come on," I said excitedly, "let's go have lunch and then we can explore."

But all our plans of going on a great hunt once we were back inside fell by the wayside when I opened the front door and came face to face with Dr. Crane. Not just Aunt Ruth's benign physician with an unfortunate name, but the actual, creepiest of creepy, child psychologist from my childhood.

"Hello, Jillian," he said, and before I could answer, and before Gil could catch me, I'd hit the floor for the third time that week with an almighty thud.

Chapter 14

"I need to stop doing that," I murmured, wincing as I opened my eyes. I'd been tucked onto a brocade couch in one of the sitting rooms next to a fireplace with a soft blanket draped over me. My neck and shoulder ached, and I'd wager my right side would be one impressive bruise before the day was over.

Morris had taken up residence across my knees and was sleeping soundly on his back with his paws in the air.

"Ah, she wakes," a familiar voice said and I felt the hair on the back of my neck rise. I struggled into a sitting position and turned to glare at the man I'd hoped to never see again as long as I lived.

He wasn't alone; Gil and Xan were seated at the table across from him, along with Estelle and Belinda. Nobody seemed particularly worried about me and I realized that they were actually all looking down at a chart that had been spread across the table.

I blinked a few times and looked away, not sure why everyone was so chummy all of a sudden, especially with the man who'd been involved in that terrible time in my life when Nanny had been sent away.

"You should see this, Jilly," Gil said, for once oblivious to my distress, "it's a whole blueprint of the house; complete with the old hidden servant's passages and everything. Good luck to us trying to find a will in this maze."

He looked up and frowned when he saw the expression on my face.

"What?" he asked in bewilderment. "What's wrong?"

But I couldn't answer him right then, I kept my eyes locked on the doctor and, pushing Morris gently aside, I slowly rose to my feet.

"What are you doing here?" I asked coldly.

"Jilly, this is Dr. Crane," Estelle said quickly, "he's Ruthie's private physician. He was able to get away early …"

"I know who he is. Or at least I thought I did. What I want to know is what he's doing here, after all this time, pretending to be a real doctor."

Dr. Crane looked at me with a slightly sad expression on his face and sighed heavily. He was older than I remembered of course and his slick black hair had turned salt and pepper. Instead of a neatly trimmed goatee, he had a full beard, and he now wore a pair of small, round glasses perched halfway down his nose. But, even with these changes, I would have recognized him anywhere. All that was missing was the bossy, arrogant sneer I remembered.

"So, you do remember me, Jillian," he said unhappily. "I'm sorry for that, I can assure you that I *am* a real doctor. I've been with the family, as was my father and my grandfather before him, for many years; all my life."

"But … but … you were a psychologist."

He cleared his throat and shrugged uncomfortably. "I'm afraid that I have to wear many hats in this business, Jillian."

"You..." I faltered, "you're a monster. You took everything from me."

"Jilly, what's going on?" Gil had risen slowly to his feet and was staring back and forth between me and the doctor, a look of anger and confusion on his face. "How do you know this man?"

I opened my mouth and then hesitated, torn between confronting this awful man and spilling all my newly discovered secrets in front of Gil. I wanted to tell him everything I'd learned, eventually, but I wasn't ready yet.

"Now, now," Belinda interrupted, standing up and coming quickly to my side. "This isn't the time to talk about the past. We can reminisce about the old days later, once the doctor has told you all about Ruth. He examined her while you were, er, resting and he agrees that we've done everything we medically can do. He knew where these maps of the house and estate were because Ruth had told him that he might need them someday. We were waiting for you to wake up, Jillian, before going over it all together. You do need to take it easier, dear; you still haven't recovered fully from your concussion."

Gil clenched his fists together, glaring between Belinda and the doctor as if deciding who he should fight.

My own drama can wait until later, I decided finally, *the important thing now is to help Ruth. But I won't let him off the hook. By the time we're done, he's going to explain, and apologize for, everything.*

"I think Ruth should go to the hospital," I said firmly.

"Oh, but Ruth would hate being in the hospital," Estelle said, wringing her hands together. "She just despises them. I don't want her spending her last ... I mean, any more time there than necessary."

"That's the truth," Belinda said sadly. "She was quite ill in her late teens and always said she'd never forgotten what an awful time she had there. She loves this house and the stables and being outdoors. We didn't want her cooped up in a big building full of strangers. But, I suppose if she's not lucid, and she doesn't know where she is anymore that it's probably the best course. She's not getting any better here as we'd hoped."

"You can't be serious," Aimee said furiously, walking in the open door with the loaded tea tray. "You can't send her away *now*."

A log in the hearth popped loudly, sending a chunk of burning ember flying onto the carpet. There was a scramble while everyone jumped up and then Gil, who was closest, scooped the smoldering wood up neatly onto the little metal dustpan and tossed it back into the fire. And when finally we looked up again the tea tray was on the table but there was no sign of Aimee.

"The poor thing," Belinda said sympathetically, "she's been devoted to Ruth. She's stayed by her side and nursed her day and night. Ruth is the closest thing she's had to a mother, I'm afraid."

"Couldn't we give her just one more day?" Estelle said, her eyes welling with tears. "We could do one last search of the house today, together, with everyone helping. If she still hasn't improved by morning, we can take her to the hospital and, er, inform her relatives tomorrow."

I hesitated, imagining the hordes of greedy extended family swooping down on the estate like screeching carrion birds ready to pluck the farm apart and sell it, piece by piece to the highest bidder. Including the horses. Including Damascus.

"I suppose one day wouldn't hurt," Xan said thoughtfully, glancing at me and Gile for confirmation.

"She's resting comfortably." Doctor Crane stood up and moved to the doorway. "She will be fine to move tomorrow. It will make no difference. Now, I must go."

Belinda stood as well and made a little beckoning motion toward me.

"Come dear, now is the time to ask your questions." I froze, feeling a wave of fear wash over me. Yes, I wanted to know what had happened but this felt so sudden, I wasn't prepared. I saw Gil start toward me and I made up my mind. "Fine," I said to Dr. Crane, "you have ten minutes." Ignoring Gil's baffled expression, I left him behind and followed Belinda and the doctor out into the hallway, not saying a word until we'd reached the front door.

"Jillian, I truly am sorry," he said, looking down at me with a sympathetic look that I wanted to slap off his face.

"I don't want your apology," I said coldly. "I only want to know one thing. Can you reverse it?"

"No," Dr. Crane said, wincing a little under my furious gaze. "But your gift was not so much erased as it was buried. In some, not all mind you but in *some*, cases the effects can wear off as the subject ages. The procedure is a delicate combination of shock therapy, hypnotism and the power of suggestion. Each, er, patient responds slightly differently to the process. And it also depends on the strength and nature of the gift that needs to be repressed."

I raised my chin, outraged at the casual way he spoke of just eliminating gifts like they were nothing.

"It also has a little to do with how willing the subject is to be part of the procedure. Your mother, for instance, was fully behind getting rid of her one gift to strengthen another. She adapted to her post-surgical life seamlessly and, apparently, without regrets."

"My mother?" I said in astonishment, "but what did she …"

"Meanwhile," the doctor went on as if I hadn't spoken. "Ruth and yourself and several other members of this branch of the family were not at all willing. You did not seem to adapt nearly so well and no second gifts became dominant enough to take the place of the first, suppressed gift. We think it's a recessive gene that your particular branch of the family—"

"Wait a second," I held up my hand to stop him. "You're saying that both my mother and Great Aunt Ruth had this done to them, too? But what on earth kinds of gifts did you erase from them?"

"The same as yours," the doctor said, looking surprised at my question, "a gift of ghosts."

And with that, he opened the front door and strode outside. And by the time I'd gathered my wits enough to realize that I had a million more questions he'd already gotten into his small, black car and sped hastily down the driveway.

Chapter 15

Belinda had been very sympathetic and had plied me with an oversized sandwich a mug of coffee to help fortify my nerves. I wouldn't stay in the kitchen to eat, though; I was too agitated to keep still. Gil found me sitting with my plate in my lap, seated on the bottom step of the winding staircase beneath the Dark Lady's stained-glass window.

"There you are," he said in a controlled voice. He sat down next to me and then reached out to snag a slice of dill pickle off my plate.

I raised an eyebrow at his thievery and then automatically slid closer so our shoulders touched.

He didn't ask me about my conversation with the doctor. He didn't pry at all. He just sat there quietly, being there for me. Like he'd always been.

"We've missed our chance to see if anything happens at nine o'clock in the morning," I said, nodding toward the multicoloured fingers of sunlight that were inching across the floor, filtered through the glass of the Dark Lady's window.

Gil nodded and glanced over at the ancient grandfather clock in the corner. "I suppose we'd better examine the clock, just in case there is something hidden there. What are you doing sitting out here anyway?"

"I'm not sure." I shrugged and looked around the room again. "Just thinking about how little I know about Ruth's life besides that she's cranky, old, and has horses. There is a whole other side of her that I didn't know existed."

"I guess that's true of everyone, really; most people only see the surface things without bothering to look deeper."

"Like Frederick. I took him at face value because he was handsome and charming. I didn't know anything about him."

"We all make mistakes, Jilly. That's how we learn and grow."

"I've also been thinking over that clue again," I said, shifting the subject to safer ground. "I was hoping inspiration would strike me."

"You know, it's only eleven o'clock. The sun couldn't have moved that far in just a couple of hours. Let's just search all the places covered by light. It's not that big an area."

"Okay," I set the empty plate aside and scrambled to my feet. 'Let's start at the window."

We climbed up the stairs to the landing and carefully ran our hands over the entire glass window, inch by inch. Then we focussed on the banisters and railings, checking in vain for hollow or hidden spots. We went down the stairs slowly, examining the carpet for clues.

"There are only seven stairs on this level," I said, going back up to the window. "Maybe we take nine steps down from where the light hits?"

"Worth a try," Gil said and we stood side by side with our backs resting against the stained glass. First, we walked downward and when we reached the floor, we tested every board, trying to see if there were hollow spots. We examined every inch of the floor that was already covered by morning light.

"Now the clock," Gil said. He carefully opened the wooden

cabinet door that protected the internal workings of the clock and we peered inside and poked here and there in the hopes of discovering some hidden compartment or something.

"Nothing," Gil said, shutting the door again.

"Let's try the second floor then," I said, gazing upward to where a little light had splashed onto the upper landing. We started at the stained-glass window again and did the same careful examination of the stairs leading upward. There wasn't much on the upper landing. Just a few fake potted plants that didn't have anything concealed inside and some small paintings that we carefully took down from their wall hooks and examined all over. Nothing anywhere.

"Well, I guess it was worth a try," Gil said, shrugging. "It's a huge house; the odds of us finding something that was meant to stay hidden are slim."

"Maybe." We went down the stairs together but when we reached the bottom, I hesitated for some reason. There had been a slight drop in temperature, just enough to make me shiver but I stopped and turned my head. Perhaps it was a faint sound that drew my attention to the space behind the stairs that led to the ballroom, or maybe it was just a feeling, but I found myself walking around the corner right toward a tile that was flush up against the back of the stairwell.

"Jilly, what are you doing?" Gil asked but I just shook my head and knelt to run my fingers along the wooden baseboard.

There was a tiny clicking sound and Gil crouched beside me, reaching out to help me lift away first a small section of baseboard and then the loose tile beneath. Underneath was a dark, hollowed-out spot that smelled faintly of damp and mildew.

"How did you know this was here?" Gil asked incredulously, shooting me a strange look.

"I have no idea," I whispered, just as surprised as he was. "I just felt like I needed to look here."

"Well, there's something in here, I think. Hang on."

He cautiously reached into the dark crevice and pulled out a small metal box. It looked ancient; spider webs clung to one side and the lock on the front had rusted completely off. It certainly didn't look like it had been hidden recently.

"Open it," I said, my heart thumping.

One hinge broke away completely as soon as he started to lift the lid so he just broke the rest of it off and set it to one side. We both leaned forward and saw that nestled inside was an aged, yellow scroll tied with a faded red ribbon.

"Wow, that looks ancient," I said, reaching out carefully to extract the scroll. The paper felt fragile beneath my fingers but I was able to gently untie the ribbon and lay the paper flat on the floor in front of us.

We knelt close together, our heads brushing together as we peered down at the yellowed paper. I was hardly able to believe what I was seeing. It was a short letter written in scrawled handwriting.

This is my last will and testament, it read, *if anything should happen to me then my estate should pass to my beloved Jacob and our daughter. I made a great mistake in giving up our beautiful child without even telling my Jacob that he was about to be a father. I can only hope that, in the long run, I have done what was best for the child. If I should pass away before I can reveal my secret to the world then all my inheritance should go toward tracking down our daughter and bringing her home. The remainder of my estate should go to her, and her descendants, and to my beloved Jacob.*

"Unbelievable," I said looking down at the elegant, looping signature. It was Great Aunt Ruth's. And it was dated from over fifty years ago. "That's right around when she would have been trying to make the Olympic team," I said breathlessly, doing the math quickly in my head.

"I guess we know now why she had to quit competing," Gil said, frowning.

"She found out she was pregnant and of course she wasn't married. It would have been an awful scandal at the time, especially in this family. Her parents must have been furious."

"Well, I guess this would be the official will unless we can find the new one," Gil said slowly. "I did not see that one coming. Do you think the others know?"

"I don't think so." I shook my head. "No, probably not. I doubt that anyone but Ruth knew. She was probably sent abroad to have the baby and I bet Jacob didn't even know that she was pregnant before he was banished. I don't know if she would have told him afterward. She must have felt so guilty. Oh, this is so sad. Poor Great Aunt Ruth." My throat closed tightly as I struggled to push back tears.

Gil laid a sympathetic hand on my shoulder. "I wonder where their daughter is then. You'd think with all Ruth's money she could have found someone to track her down after all this time. If they couldn't find her then that means Jacob inherits everything."

"I don't know. Maybe she'd passed away already or didn't want anything to do with Ruth."

"I guess we should keep this somewhere safe," Gil said. "Want me to hide it in my room?"

"Sure, I don't know where else to put it, though I'm not sure if anything is exactly *safe* in this house."

In the end, Gil took it back to his room and zipped it into the lining of his travelling bag. We would wait until Ruth had been safely deposited at the hospital before going to the lawyer with our discovery. It still didn't sit with me easily, though. I'd discovered the old will by fluke, or had been mysteriously led to it anyway, but it didn't fit in with the 'lady rides nine' clue that Great Aunt Ruth had whispered to me so urgently. Was there was still something more she'd wanted us to know? Or had it just been the ramblings of a crazy old lady?

We searched the house for the entire rest of the day, even

exploring the myriad of secret passages that were on the floorplan.

"I didn't even know that half of these existed," Belinda said as we trekked down yet another dusty, cob-webbed passage. They were everywhere; some had not been used for many years, while others had scuff marks in the dust like they'd been recently travelled.

And while it was interesting to explore them all, by the time the late afternoon rolled around we were all filthy and exhausted. And no closer to finding any of Ruthie's missing wills.

Chapter 16

"Do you want to come with me while I work with Damascus?" I asked Gil later that afternoon. "I thought I'd bring him in and brush him one final time and say goodbye."

We'd decided to pack up and head for home the next morning once Ruth had been admitted to the hospital and we'd shared what we knew with the lawyer. Nobody felt comfortable staying at the estate any longer under the circumstances.

We also wanted to be well out of the house before the swarms of relatives descended. I planned to let the lawyer know that I wanted to buy Damascus and hopefully, whichever relative inherited would accept my meager offer. The lawyer could also let me know if the colt ended up being shipped to auction instead and I could try to make a bid on him there. It was a tentative plan at best, but at least it gave me a little hope.

"No, you go ahead. I'm going to pack and get the horse trailer ready for tomorrow."

"Alright." I watched him go with a frown, noticing the tense line of his shoulders. He had grown steadily more withdrawn the closer the time came for our departure. I wished I knew what he was thinking. I honestly had no idea what I was going to do once we were back at Greystone. I knew things couldn't just go back to normal between me and my parents. There was so much that they had to answer for.

Bally lifted his head and marched right up to the gate when he saw me, Damascus following closely behind.

I fed them each an apple and then slid Damascus's halter on and led him from the pasture.

"Don't worry, Bally," I said, "I'm just going to brush the little guy and then I'll be back for you."

Bally snorted and then dropped his head to nibble at the grass growing near the fence, following us with his gaze. I felt a twinge of guilt and pushed it away. I had the whole rest of my life to spend with Bally and maybe only a few short hours left to spend with Damascus; I wanted to make the most of it.

Still, I turned to look over my shoulder to find my horse watching us with an uncharacteristically anxious look on his face.

"I'll be back for you in an hour," I promised, ignoring the uneasy feeling in the pit of my stomach.

Damascus followed me peacefully to the barn and clopped down the aisle to his stall. I left him there working on a pile of fresh hay while I went to the tack room to find some brushes. My grooming tote was where I'd left it, on a lower shelf just inside the doorway and I leaned in to get it just as a cold breeze gusted down the aisle, sending an unnatural shiver through my entire body.

Damascus neighed loudly from his stall and there was a crashing noise as he threw himself against his stall door, his eyes rolling wildly in panic.

The Curse of The Golden Touch

"You're okay," I said, hurrying toward him. "Easy buddy, you're fine."

I slid his stall door open, stepping in and closing myself inside while I waited for him to calm down. I looked around in dismay at the trampled bedding that had been churned and pawed up into uneven mounds. He'd been alone for less than a minute and he'd already knocked another chunk of stone out of the wall near his manger; bits of broken rock lay scattered nearby.

"Silly horse, I was only gone for two seconds, you didn't have to destroy the place," I said, sighing as I went to comfort him. I didn't like that he'd gotten himself so worked up over nothing. A young horse with a naturally anxious temperament wasn't something I looked for in a prospect. They might be prone to colic, or other ailments, or might not be able to handle the pressure of travelling from show to show.

He's just a baby, I told myself, but there was a part of me that was disappointed that he didn't have the same naturally calm temperament as the perfect Bally. What I'd seen so far from Damascus had led me to believe that he was a steady-eddie type of horse who didn't get overly fussed by much so this was a bit of a let-down.

"Come on, friend, this is supposed to be fun. I'm just going to get you brushed and then we'll go for a walk and find you some nice grass to graze on. But you have to calm down and let me brush you first."

There was a soft thumping noise from the direction of the tack room and Damascus snorted and threw up his head, his ears pricked anxiously in that direction.

The temperature dropped. I looked up slowly, prickling all over with the sudden, uncomfortable feeling that I was being watched from the shadows.

All the hair on the back of my neck stood on end as another icy little breeze raced down the aisle, ruffling the straw bedding and the colt's fluffy mane and tail. For a second, I saw a flash of red out of the corner of my eye, right at the back of Damascus's stall. But when I turned my head, nothing was there.

Shivering, I reached out and laid a reassuring hand on the little colt's neck, but I wasn't sure if it was to calm him or myself.

Stop being such a baby, there's nobody there, I told myself firmly. *It's just the wind or maybe Gil slipped in somehow and is getting our stuff ready in the tack room.*

"Hello," I called out, making an effort to keep my voice steady. "Gil? Is anyone there?" But there was no answer. Somewhere down near the far end of the barn a stall door rattled in the breeze, rolling back and forth rhythmically with a metallic grating sound.

Damascus squealed in alarm and half-reared in the air, striking his little front foot at the place in the wall he'd already half-demolished. His hoof hit the crumbling rock with a sickening crunch and I jumped forward and pushed my hands into his chest, backing him into the middle of his stall.

"That's enough of that," I told him firmly, pulling on his halter. "You stop that nonsense right now. You'll hurt yourself."

Another door began to rattle, this time closer and then another one, the noise loud enough to set my teeth on edge. I had no idea of what was happening but it felt like more than just a normal wind.

"Was it the Dark Lady again? Was she angry that we hadn't figured out her cryptic clue?

"I'm sorry," I called out, feeling a little silly, "we did the best we could." Maybe if my gift hadn't been stolen from me, I would have been able to communicate with her better.

The wind died right down and I heaved a sigh of relief. Then there was a loud bang and all the doors began to rattle at once and the temperature plummeted.

"All right, Damascus," I said with false brightness, masking my spiking anxiety. We needed to get out of there. Fast. "Everything is fine. Let's just go outside for a walk. There's a good boy."

Damascus didn't need to be told twice. I barely had time to clip his lead rope on before he'd barged forward and practically towed me out into the aisle, his hooves clattering on the stone floor. I didn't usually let horses pull me around, but in this case, I wanted to get out of there just as much as he did. I hurried after him out into the sunshine.

The second we were outside, the noise behind us stopped. Damascus heaved a deep breath, snorting and nudging me with his nose. I wrapped my arm around his neck and gave him a tight hug.

"What on earth was that?" I asked him, rubbing him reassuringly on the withers. Was it just the weird winds that ran around this place or had it been the Dark Lady trying to tell me something? Either way, I was glad we were leaving this strange place tomorrow.

Damascus walked along gently beside me like a lamb as I led him along the overgrown trail that led around the outside edge of the pastures. As soon as we reached the one Bally was in, he came trotting up to meet us, nickering anxiously under his breath and reaching his nose out to touch me and the little colt over and over again. It was like he was reassuring himself that we were okay.

I did a big loop of the trails and then circled back to the gate where Bally was, once again, waiting for us. I let Damascus inside the pasture, expecting him to gallop away but instead, he and Bally both came over to me and stood close, each one gently laying their noses on my left and right shoulder, their warm breath washing over me from both sides. I stood stone-still, not sure what was happening but also not wanting to break the spell. Finally, they each gave me a little nudge, and then turned and walked away together like nothing had happened.

Sometimes I think the longer I work with horses the less I know about them, I thought, watching the two of them leave. Just when I thought I had them all figured out they'd do something completely out of the blue to surprise me. One thing was for sure, they were smarter and more intuitive than most people gave them credit for.

Chapter 17

The rest of the afternoon passed peacefully enough. Gil finished packing the trailer and Xan and I got our suitcases ready. Xan was still moody and withdrawn.

He's still very hurt that Estelle lied to him, I thought sympathetically, *I know how awful that feels.*

I also knew that the thing that would help him most was the time to process things in his own way.

We took turns sitting at Ruth's bedside, although she didn't wake up again. She looked peaceful though, and I hoped we were doing the right thing by sending her to the hospital.

The three of us kept ourselves busy until it was time to bring the horses in from the pasture for dinner. The barn felt perfectly normal now, not frightening at all. I was almost tempted to believe that the whole thing had been my imagination. Almost, but not quite.

Damascus had completely recovered from his earlier scare. He ate his hay tranquilly while I set to work tidying the stall he'd dismantled, shoving the loose rock back into his wall again and cleaned the scatted bits of rock and plaster out of the straw.

"I'm going to hate leaving you behind, little guy, even if you are a goof," I told him, hugging his thin neck.

There was an hour or so to wait before dinner time so I decided to head to the library to finish what I could of that awful book. It might be the last chance I had to read it, although if Belinda was right then there should have been a copy handed down to Mother, too. When I got home there were a lot of things she was going to have to answer for. Whole chunks of my life were missing and I wanted some pretty detailed explanations.

The hearth was already laid out so I made a fire and sat back in one of the deep leather chairs with the book open in my lap, looking for the paragraph where I'd stopped reading last.

Oh, right, there it is, I thought with a sigh, *Alocious is going off again about how to use gifts to cheat people out of their land and businesses. He had a one-track mind, and not an ounce of scruples.*

I read a bit more and then set the book down abruptly with a sigh. It was my family history, it was important for me to read and yet I could barely stand a single word that flowed from this awful man's pen. There had to be a better way to know the truth about people like me. Belinda had hinted that not all families had been corrupted like mine. Maybe I would travel overseas and find some distant cousins to visit once I left Greystone, maybe that would help everything make sense.

I gazed dreamily into the flickering flames. There was something soothing and hypnotic about them that made me feel safe and secure. I let my gaze drift lazily around the room, staring idly at the old pictures and paintings that decorated the wall.

The one closest to me was the old painting that showed the stables before the new addition had been put on. Back when it had been just the stone barn with only a handful of stalls, a cobblestoned aisle way, and strangely dressed grooms wearing serious expressions.

The barn was empty of horses except for one chestnut hunter that stood fully tacked up in the last stall with his head over the door.

That red horse sure looks like the one the dark lady rode in my dream, I thought. *He's even wearing a side-saddle. I suppose there's a chance it could be the same one as in the stained-glass window. Evangeline did live here, after all. I wonder how old the painting is. It looks ancient.*

I picked up the book again to read and then set it down in my lap with a little cry.

That ends right where Damascus's stall must be right now, I thought excitedly, hardly daring to trust where my wild thoughts were leading. Surely, I couldn't be right. It was too simple.

I got up and went to the painting, counting the stalls from the front to the end. *There are nine*, I thought in wonder. Why hadn't I seen it before? I thought of the crumbling wall and the sound of the little colt's hoof hitting the rock, a low *hollow* sound. I'd replaced that rock *twice* for heaven's sake. How dense a person was I to have missed it?

"Hello, Jillian," Aimee said from the doorway.

I jerked in surprise and spun around. "Oh, you scared me."

"Sorry," she said, flashing her teeth in a bright smile, "you were a million miles away, I guess. What are you doing?"

For a second, I thought about sharing everything with her. "Oh, nothing," I said, shrugging as casually as I could manage. "Just studying the paintings. I love art, don't you?"

"Not particularly. Come, sit down. I brought you tea."

"Thank you. You didn't have to do that." I went reluctantly back to my chair and sat down obediently. The habit of always automatically doing what I was told was going to be a hard one to break.

"We're cousins, Aimee. I don't expect you to wait on me."

"Don't you?" she said, setting the tea tray down on the table with a sharp clatter. "But you expect *someone* to serve you, right? There's always someone to bring you things and clean up your messes back at your house, isn't there?"

"Well, yes, I suppose so," I admitted. "But that's not my fault. I was just born into that house. I don't have any say in how it's run. And besides, I'm not staying there much longer; as soon as I get home and figure out a plan, Gil and I are leaving Greystone. I'm starting my life over on my terms. I'm sick of living in my mother's shadow."

"Are you?" She looked startled and then a red blush crawled up her neck and stained her cheeks. She looked away and for a second, I almost thought she had tears in her eyes.

"You're a nice person, Jilly. I'm sorry we didn't have time to get to know one another. If things had turned out differently, I'm sure we could have been friends. Goodbye."

"We're not leaving until tomorrow—" I started to say, but she turned on her heel and left before I could get the words out.

"That's strange," I said to the empty room and looked eagerly back to the painting. As soon as everyone was in bed I would have to go out and see if my guess was right. I couldn't leave a mystery like that until morning.

Suddenly, I noticed the most delicious smell rising from the teapot. Hints of cinnamon, cloves and ginger, and something dark and sweet that made me think of long winter nights curled up cozily by the fire while snow drifted down outside. I took a deep, relaxing breath; the scent was intoxicating and bewitching. All the urgency, the sense of importance I'd just felt, drifted away.

Maybe I'll just have a small cup of this before dinner, I thought languidly, pouring the delicious smelling brew into the delicate teacup that sat beside the matching pot.

I'd just raised the cup to my lips and taken the tiniest sip when the door burst open with a bang and Morris tore into the room, his orange fur puffed up crazily in all directions so he looked like an enraged jack-o-lantern.

"Morris! What on earth?"

But, before I could stop him, he yowled and leapt straight toward me with his claws out. He smashed the cup out of my hand as he flew past and skidded across the table beside me, knocking the entire tea tray to the carpet with a mighty clatter.

I screamed and leapt to my feet, watching in horror as he tore around the room, leaping and hissing like he was possessed. He finally bolted past me and shot back out into the hall. I could hear him yowling all the way down the corridor.

I looked down at the smashed tea things in dismay, watching the dark liquid run in rivulets across the carpet and onto the hardwood floor. The intoxicating smell of tea filled the room for a moment and then drifted away completely

I need to find something to clean this up. A glance around the room told me that I would need to go to the kitchen to find cleaning supplies. I almost rang the bell to call Aimee but then remembered what she'd said about me needing servants to do everything for me. No, I was perfectly capable of doing things for myself.

There was no sign of Morris when I came out into the hall. I had no idea what had come over the poor thing but I'd find him and make sure he was feeling better as soon as I cleared the mess away.

The hallway was empty but the heavenly smells of dinner cooking floated down from the kitchen and I headed that way, my mouth watering. I would miss Belinda's cooking something fierce when I went back to Greystone.

At first glance the kitchen was empty, pots bubbled quietly

on the stove and the oven light was on, but Belinda was nowhere in sight.

"Hello," I called, "sorry to bother you but…"

There was a low thumping sound from the dining room down the hall and I turned that way, feeling that cold, prickling sensation on my neck again. Reluctantly, I went to the half-open doorway and stepped inside.

I stopped dead in the entrance to the dining room, putting a hand over my mouth to stifle the scream trying to escape. The table was laid out perfectly and half the chairs were occupied. Gil was there and Xan. So were Belinda, Jacob and Estelle. But instead of eating or talking, everyone just sat immobile, staring straight ahead, eyes open, unmoving.

"Gil!" I cried, rushing to his side. He didn't move, he just sat like a rock, his eyes staring vacantly into the air in front of him. I reached out to him, searching for trembling fingers for a pulse, my own heart beating wildly.

There, there it was. Faint but steady. I gave him a frantic shake but he didn't so much as blink.

I went in turn to everyone at the table nearly crying with relief when I realized they were all alive; at least for now.

"Help," said a weak voice from the kitchen, "please help."

"I'm coming." I ran to the kitchen and found Aimee sprawled out on the floor, blood oozing from a cut on her temple.

"Oh, Aimee, are you hurt? What happened?"

"It's … the doctor. It was Dr. Crane all this time. He's in the house and he has a gun. I tried to stop him but he hit me and he … he's bewitched the others somehow. He said he's after Ruth's will. He went upstairs and I'm afraid he's hurting her."

"Aimee, where's the phone. We have to call the police."

"I tried that. The line is dead, he must have cut it. Do hurry, Jilly. There's not much time left. He said that he'd kill everyone including Ruth unless he gets what he wants. He's convinced that we found the will and are keeping it from him. I don't know what to do."

"Don't worry, Aimee," I said quickly, "I know where it is, or at least I think I do. Come on, lean on me and we'll go together. I can't leave you here alone."

A look of anguish flashed across her face and she slumped, putting her head in her hands. "No, no. I'll be all right; I'd just slow you down. You have to hurry, though. Go get help."

Not stopping, I flew down the hall and out the front door as fast as I could, my feet racing across the half-frozen lawn. The clouds had scudded away and now the moon was out, shining over me and lighting up the path to the barn as if it were daylight.

The horses looked up from their hay, blinking at the sudden light. I flew to Damascus's stall and slipped inside, patting him reassuringly before I knelt in the thick straw bedding.

I felt the loose spot carefully with my fingertips and gently pried the biggest rock free, letting it tumble into the straw. Behind it was a hollowed-out hiding place that must have been built right into the wall when it was constructed. Inside was a metal box much like the one Gil and I had found earlier but newer looking as if it had been freshly buried.

It wasn't locked and I lifted the lid with shaking fingers, pulling out the scroll with a sense of unreality. *All this drama for a silly piece of paper.* The thick parchment was brand new and unrolled easily when I untied the bright red ribbon. I read it, my eyes widening in astonishment as I committed the brief contents of the will to memory just in case I needed to tell the police later what was in it.

The front barn door creaked in the wind, and I clutched the will tightly to my chest protectively.

I paused in the aisle, not sure what to do next. I had the

will; did I go up to the house and try and reason with a killer, a madman, hoping he was reasonable enough to spare everyone's lives if I gave him what he wanted? Or did I escape now and find a way to call the police and hope that they could get here in time to save Gil and everyone else?

It was an awful choice and I stood frozen, my heart pounding, unable to make a decision either way.

It was finally Bally who decided for me. He nickered loudly and stuck his head over his stall door, grasping the latch in his teeth just like he did when he let himself out at Greystone. He carefully worked the latch until it popped free and the door slid gently open.

All right, we'll ride for help then, I thought, *there were more farms up the road; we passed them on the way. I'll ride to one of those and use the phone to call the police.*

"Good boy, Bally," I whispered, pulling his halter off the stall door and slipping it over his head. I fastened the tail-end of the lead rope to his halter to make a set of rough reins and led him quietly out into the moonlight.

I'll have to climb the fence to get on him, I thought, hugging the shadowy side of the barn as we headed in the direction of the driveway. I wished that his silvery coat didn't glow quite so brightly in the moonlight; he looked like he was lit up from within.

"Going somewhere, Jillian?" a cold voice said behind me.

I froze, caught like a rabbit in headlights and then slowly turned around.

"Alastair?" I said in confusion, taking a second to recognize my cousin. He looked much different than the last time I'd seen him. Older, his features sharper and harder than I remembered. "Thank goodness you're here. You have to help. The doctor is holding everyone hostage." My voice died away as I took in the expression on his face.

My relief on seeing that it was Xan's creepy brother rather than the even creepier Dr. Crane was short-lived.

"Hello, Jilly," Alastair said, tilting his head a little to one side, a smile playing over his lips. "I bet you're surprised to see me."

"What ... what are you doing here?"

"Oh, just tying up some loose ends. I believe you have something that I want. Hand it over."

I stared at him. "You ... you want the will? But why? I thought Dr. Crane—"

"That old quack is safe in bed at his own home, Jillian. He has nothing to do with this. And I want the will to destroy it, of course."

"But ... but why?" I asked, completely bewildered by this turn of events.

"You're certainly not the sharpest tool in the shed, are you?" Alastair said, laughing under his breath. "I'd almost hoped someone would have figured it out by now. You have no idea how lonely it is always being the cleverest man in the room, Jilly. It's not easy being brilliant."

"I don't understand what's going on at all," I said, edging Bally a few steps away from him toward the shadow of the barn. "Ruth's will doesn't even list you as a beneficiary. Why would you want it?"

"No, of course *that* will doesn't, my poor, innocent, dim-witted cousin; that's why it needs to be destroyed. You just hand it over and we'll burn it like we did the others. Ruth thought she could escape me by writing all those wills, but I was too smart for her. I found the one I wanted and then destroyed the rest one by one. Nobody outwits me."

"But, how did you know she was writing them?"

"I am a very special man, Jilly, I don't think there's another like me in the whole world. I can be anywhere I want if I think about it hard enough, or at least a part of me can. Enough so that I can watch and listen and learn people's secrets. I can even influence them to do what I want when the conditions are right."

"Really?" I asked, wondering if I'd somehow fallen into a dream, a nightmare. "Belinda said Great Aunt Ruth thought someone was watching her. Was that you all that time?"

"Of course. Old Ruthless is a little more perceptive than the average person. She could feel me watching. She resisted my suggestions and I'm afraid I needed to use a little more force than necessary to get her to write exactly the will I needed. It only worked once and she wrote all those other ones too, the poor thing. She was very confused by the time I was done with her. She thought hiding them all would stop me."

"But why would Ruth leave the estate to you? Everyone is going to suspect the truth if you're her beneficiary. She made it no secret that she—"

"Hated me? No, she was quite vocal about that. No, my simple, simple little cousin, the will lists Xan as the sole heir, not me. I'm not an idiot."

"Xan," I whispered, feeling the crushing weight of disappointment. Had he been in on it all that time?

"Aw, cheer up. My simpleton of a brother doesn't know anything about it. I just needed him to inherit for a month or so. And then he'll have a tragic accident on that unpredictable horse of his and it will all be mine. Did you know that even some animals are susceptible to my influence, Jillian? Some minds are so easy to manipulate. Now, set that will down there nice and easy on the ground, and then you and I will go for a little walk."

He pulled a gun out and leveled it at me, a twisted expression of joy on his face. I froze, holding my breath and eyeing the gun with mounting terror. I needed to stall for time. I needed to come up with a plan. Quickly.

There was a puff of warm breath on my arm and I glanced sideways to see that Bally had crept up behind me and was standing right at my back.

Chapter 18

"Why are you doing this, Alastair?" I said tearfully, turning to stare transfixed at the barrel of the gun. I pressed backward into Bally's solid warmth, letting him infuse me with strength. There had to be a way out of this *somehow*.

"Why shouldn't I get what's mine?" Alastair demanded. "I deserve more than anyone to have this estate and all the wealth that goes with it. When my feeble-minded parents lost everything, I knew that it would be up to me to make my own fortune."

"But you have an estate—"

"Ha, that crumbling old ruin. No, we're in debt up to our eyeballs, Jillian. We're about to be out on the street, penniless and abandoned by every relative we have, no doubt. I couldn't let that happen to Sally and me, not after all we've sacrificed to get ahead."

"What ... what do you mean?"

"Everyone shrinks away from the children of a failing, penniless man, Jillian. When our parents were poor but still alive, we were like pariahs, bathed in the stink of some contagious disease. But an orphan is a different story altogether. Being parentless gave us the opportunities we needed; it had to be done."

"What had to be done? You mean ... your parents?"

"I am not without remorse, Jillian. I'll admit that my mother had her good points. But unfortunately, she had to go, too. She knew too much. I don't think they suffered."

"Oh, Alastair," I said, "that is awful."

"No," he said coldly, leveling the gun at my heart, "what is awful is parents squandering your fortune. No bad deed goes unpunished, Jillian. So now, dear cousin, I'm afraid your time is up. You should have drunken your damn tea and sat in the library like a good little girl. Instead, you had to ruin everything once again. We just needed a few more nights and Ruth would have been worn down enough to tell us where the will was. But you had to stick your nose in and involve the doctor. We couldn't have that Jilly. I'm sure you understand. Now, you're going to have a little accident as well."

"Oh, please, Alastair, don't do this. Lots of people know where I am. You won't get away with killing me."

"Oh, I think I will. When the others wake up, they won't remember a thing. You'll just be missing and later they'll find your body at the bottom of that canyon. They'll just assume you fell off it because you're an idiot who couldn't keep from nosing around in the dark where she doesn't belong."

"Aimee," I said slowly, stalling for time. I backed Bally another step toward the shadows. "She helped you, didn't she? She must have known about this all along."

"Well, of course she did. She's a perfect genius with potions and she had the opportunity. She's a bit of a lost soul though; it didn't take much to convince her to help me."

"But she loved Ruth. How did you get her to betray her?"

"Money," Alastair said with a shrug. "Jealousy. Aren't those the keys to everyone's allegiance? Once you tell someone that they deserve more than life's given them, they come around pretty quickly. She was putty in my hands."

"The police will figure it out, Alastair," I said, grasping at straws. "Everything will lead back to you when you inherit the estate."

"Nobody even knows I'm here, Jillian. I'm hundreds of miles away, tucked safely at home in my warm bed. I will be woken up tomorrow by Xan informing me of Ruth's tragic demise and that our poor, stupid cousin is missing. Aimee will arrange to have the will found, of course, and then everything will fall into place."

Whatever hope was still beating frantically away inside me faded away and I stood there, cold and shivering, certain I was about to die at any second.

"Right, well, as pleasant as this has been, it's time for you to say goodbye, Jillian. Start walking."

Bally pricked his ears as there was the slightest crackling in the bushes behind Alastair. I saw Aimee walking slowly toward us, frowning at the gun in Alastair's hand. The wound on her head was gone and I wondered if it had been fake or had somehow already healed. Alastair jerked his head up and smiled a slow, sultry smile when he saw her.

I had a moment of inspiration. "Do you know what this last will says?" I asked loudly.

"No." Alastair shrugged. "And I don't care. I'm just going to burn it."

"Well, maybe Aimee cares. Ruth left the entire estate to her."

There was a moment of tense silence.

"To me?" Aimee asked in surprise. "Why?"

"Didn't you know, Aimee? You're her granddaughter."

"No," Aimee gasped, putting a hand over her mouth. "No, I'm not. My parents died in a fire; I know my grandparents."

"Those people adopted you when you were a baby, Aimee. It says right here in the will. Ruth and Jacob had a child out of wedlock when they were just teenagers; your mother. Ruth's parents forced her to give up the baby and banished her from seeing Jacob but she always regretted it. Many years later she tracked down her daughter, but the woman was angry and bitter and didn't want anything to do with her. Shortly after, she became pregnant with her own child but wasn't in a position to keep her. She didn't want Ruth's help, but Ruth secretly used her influence to make sure the baby was placed with kind, very distant relatives. She knew who you were, Aimee. She was just waiting for the right time to tell you. Look, it's all here in the will."

I reached up and slowly pulled the document from where I'd shoved it in my sleeve; holding it out to her.

"Don't listen to that drivel, Aimee, she's lying."

"I'm not, and if Alastair is as good at lurking around corners and eavesdropping as he says then he would have known the truth already, too."

Aimee looked stricken, her gaze wavering uncertainly between me, the will, and Alastair.

"Go on, read it," I said boldly, "and then ask yourself why your boyfriend didn't tell you and also why he didn't just let you inherit and then marry you since he supposedly loves you so much."

"That's enough out of you," Alastair snarled, marching toward me. Still waving the gun in my face, he snatched the will out of my hand and crumpled it into a ball.

"Don't!" Aimee cried out. "I want to read it first. I deserve to read it if it's mine."

"You deserve nothing," Alastair spat, "you're worthless without me."

"I'm not," Aimee protested, but her eyes welled with tears and she dropped her gaze to the ground.

"She isn't," I said hotly, "and this is a much better plan. Aimee, when you inherit you can just share the money with Alastair. After all, that's what he was planning to do with you, right? You were going to split the money?"

"I … I think so," Aimee said miserably, looking anxiously toward Alastair. "If I did everything he said. And I did do everything right, darling, or almost everything. Now that it's almost over, we can be together forever like we planned."

"You would have messed it up completely if it wasn't for me," Alastair snarled. "You were supposed to use your potions to put Ruth in a hypnotized state so she'd tell you where all the bloody, hidden wills were, not knock her out for months. You're the one that's killed her, Aimee, your own grandmother, too. No, it's best if I inherit and take care of the money since I'm smart enough to handle it. You'll get a small share, of course; you've been a loyal servant."

"Servant?" Aimee said, moving toward him. "But, Alastair, I love—"

"None of that," he snapped. "Never mind, you're right, this is better. I'll take care of two birds with one stone and finish this properly. Then Sally and I can have it all for ourselves and live in the manner we deserve."

"What are you talking about?" she asked, stricken.

"Dividing things up is such a bore. I guess you'll just all have to disappear. Oh well."

Alistair brought the gun up and pointed directly at Aimee's head, with no trace of remorse in his cold eyes.

An incredulous look passed over Aimee's face and suddenly, she wasn't scared anymore. She looked angry. Deadly angry.

She clenched both hands together and glared at Alastair. The air around her seemed to flicker and glow with an otherworldly light.

Alastair's eyes widened and he took a couple of uncertain steps backward. "Aimee," he said uncertainly. "Stop that. What are you doing?"

She didn't answer but the look on her face grew even more murderous.

Alastair gave a sharp cry of pain and nearly dropped the gun, moving it from hand to hand as if it had turned burning hot.

"What are you doing?" he cried. "Stop that."

He levelled the gun in her direction and squeezed the trigger hard, four times in a row. The sound was awful, a low cracking sound that echoed off the barn. Aimee fell like a tree in the forest, slowly rocking back on her heels with a look of startled wonder on her face before she crashed against the ground. She let out an anguished cry, shuddered once, and then went quite still.

"No," I cried. "Aimee, no!"

I started to move forward but Alastair pointed the gun in my direction, his face twisted with rage.

"I wanted this to be neat and tidy, Jillian, but you had to poke your nose in and ruin things for everyone. Thanks to you, I have *two* bodies to dispose of. You couldn't have just walked nicely to the edge of the precipice yourself like you were supposed to, could you? Do you realize what a selfish, spoiled brat you are? You never think of anyone but yourself."

He's completely crazy, I thought, as if this was a new insight given the events of the evening. But looking at his manic expression, I realized that Alastair believed everything he was saying.

"Well, if you won't walk then I guess I'll just have to finish you off here," he snarled.

Three things happened almost all at once. There was a strange crackling, popping noise from the place where Aimee had fallen. For a moment, I could see her lying there just as she had been and in the next moment, she had disappeared completely, vanished in the night. Alastair jerked the gun up wildly and let out a surprised cry.

That was my opportunity but before I could turn and push Bally away to safety, Alastair turned on me again and jammed his finger against the trigger. There was a blazing, burning, shattering feeling in my arm and I staggered backward, falling against Bally's trembling side.

Oh, that's funny ... the sound comes later, I thought fuzzily as the crackle and bang of the gun sounded a full second after the pain. Then Bally was leaping forward, knocking me roughly to the ground and there were more bangs and someone was screaming in a high wail that seemed to echo from inside my head.

There was utter blackness, and then when my eyes opened again, the sound of sirens cut through the night, still far away but heading steadily in my direction.

I sat up with a groan, clutching my ruined arm to my chest. Every breath was agony, but that was nothing compared to what I felt when I caught sight of Alastair and Bally.

Oh, Bally, I choked back a sob and crawled over to where he lay, his body almost obliterating the smaller form of Alastair below. *Oh no, this can't be happening.*

They both lay there, unmoving; Alastair with his blue eyes staring sightlessly up at the stars and Bally with his eyes gently closed as if he were peacefully sleeping. But he wasn't sleeping; the large wounds in his great, wonderful heart were all the answers I needed. He was unbelievably gone. Just like that.

Oh, Bally, you can't leave me alone. I can't face a world without you. And then I began to cry.

I couldn't have sat there for long but it felt like an eternity. I struggled to my feet as the sirens came closer, not wanting to see anyone right then, not wanting to see them take Bally away or stand around staring at his lifeless body. I limped toward the safety of the forest and kept going until the lights and sounds faded far behind and the blessed silence of the woods closed in on me.

Finally, I stumbled on the roots of an enormous tree and when I fell, I just lay there, curling myself tightly into a ball with my head resting on a gnarled outcropping. The moon came out from behind another cloud and rose high above me, looking larger and much more important than usual. There was a rustling sound next to my ear and then a gentle puff of warm air caressed my cheek.

"Bally?" I said incredulously, pushing myself upright to stare with disbelieving eyes. Maybe I was dreaming or hallucinating from blood loss because there he was, shining splendidly in the moonlight without a mark on him. There was no gaping hole in his chest, and he'd lost his halter and lead rope somewhere.

I looked down at my blood-smeared clothing and felt the sharp lingering pain in my side. No, I was definitely awake, but then how was this possible? Was it a miracle?

He nickered and touched my side carefully as if he were asking me how badly I was hurt.

Suddenly, I didn't care how crazy this was, I was only glad to have my horse back again.

I reached out to wrap my good arm around his nose in a hug, and that was when the awful reality of my situation hit me full force. To my horror, my hand passed right through him as if he wasn't even there.

"Oh no, Bally," I said, putting a hand over my eyes to hold back the tears. "This can't be happening."

He stared at me patiently and snorted, looking at me with his normal wide, intelligent eyes. He didn't seem disturbed at all.

No, this couldn't be real; he was not a ghost. The shock of Alastair trying to kill me and everyone else had sent me around the bend. Losing Bally was bad, but going crazy and thinking I was seeing Bally alive was even worse.

A branch cracked somewhere nearby and I opened my eyes, on high alert. What if Alastair had somehow survived after all and was not back there by the barn lying under Bally's crushing weight? I held my breath and scanned the moonlit woods, waiting.

A translucent, flickering figure entered the little grove and I shrank back, not ready to face any more trauma that night.

"Jilly?" The voice was light, wavery and definitely Scottish. I pulled myself painfully to a sitting position, now sure that I was dead or at least hallucinating.

"Nanny," I asked incredulously. "Is it really you?"

"Of course it is, dear," she said faintly. Her flickering image grew stronger the closer she got to me and Bally and soon I could see her familiar face looking exactly as I remembered her all those years before. She'd hardly aged at all since I saw her and the loving look on her face nearly undid me.

"Oh, Nanny," I cried, not caring anymore if this was all a figment of my imagination. "Oh, you're back. You've come back for me."

"I never left you, silly child. I've been with you all this time."

"You mean, you're ... dead?" I asked tentatively, stating the obvious.

"I'm afraid so. I had a heart attack and passed away a few months after I left Greystone. I couldn't bear leaving my wee girl and I think my heart just broke. But I've been watching over you all this time, darling, waiting for the time when you'd be able to see me again."

"I'm so sorry, Nanny," I sobbed, "I couldn't see the ghosts anymore. I didn't know you were there."

"That's all right, darling, the main thing is that you can now. Your kind doesn't do well when part of their gift is severed. The power is tied to you like a life force, and without your gift, you sort of dry up and become brittle inside. Like your mother; like your Aunt Ruth."

"I'm nothing like my mother," I spat out angrily. "She was a monster for what she did to me."

"Yes, but she was young once and very much like you, Jillian."

"She squandered her gift on purpose. I didn't have a choice."

"Sometimes our choices are subtle, Jillian. The choice to get along, to not cause trouble even at our own expense, the choice to fit in rather than accept our gifts."

I gulped. I supposed a tiny part of me had had a choice when I was a teenager. I could have run away with Gil. I could have fought harder.

I closed my eyes in resignation but opened them quickly when I felt a sharp tap on my shoulder.

"Wake up, Jillian," Nanny said, tapping me again. "Your mother did a wicked thing when she suppressed your gift, but you don't have the luxury of being a helpless victim of circumstance anymore. You are not to blame for what happened to you when you were a child. But you are responsible for the here and now. You could have had your powers back a long time ago if you'd chosen to fight for them … to fight for *you*. Your Nanny didn't teach you to back down from a fight, did she?"

"No," I said in a small voice, remembering belatedly how feisty and bossy Nanny had been when she'd been alive. Death hadn't mellowed that trait very much.

"Now get up on your feet, Jillian. Hard times are coming for you, and maybe some good times, too, so it's time to get up and look life full in the face. It's time for you to go back, Jillian, back to Greystone. You have things to do there before you head out on your own. And things to learn too. I'll be waiting for you there."

The last thing I wanted to do was get back to my feet. The mixture of being overwhelmed and blood loss was nearly too much. I wanted nothing more than to just curl up and sleep for weeks.

Bally looked up from where he was pretending to graze with his translucent teeth and pricked his ears in my direction.

My eyes watered and my throat closed just looking at him; never, never would I be able to pet my beautiful horse again. He was lost to me forever. Soon, he would fade and disappear to whatever place good horses went when they died.

I closed my eyes again, washed in misery, only to open them again with a yelp as ghost-Bally nudged me sharply in the side.

"Hey, stop that, Bally," I said, holding my side in surprise. How was he able to touch me when my hand had gone right through him earlier?

"Stop wasting time, Jillian," Nanny said sharply. "That horse isn't going to leave you alone until you stand up and get yourself to safety. You've lost a lot of blood. You won't last much longer if you go on like this."

"Fine," I sighed tiredly. "I'm going, I'm going."

But it wasn't that easy. I clambered to my feet and stumbled blindly through the woods in the direction I thought I'd come but the trees all looked the same now. My legs shook underneath me, barely strong enough to hold me up. I couldn't move my right arm and I had to keep it cradled against my side to keep the throbbing, pulsing ache at bay.

Bally followed me calmly, reaching out his head and neck ever so often to steady me or steer me in a slightly different direction. Those touches hurt almost as much as the bullet had because each one reminded me of my loss, and when I reached out to him tentatively again there was only air.

He lifted his head and nickered softly. Up ahead came an answering snort and a blood-red horse came out of the forest, his ears pricked and his eyes no longer filled with the urgency they'd seemed to hold before.

The rider on his back looked softer, too. She smiled at me gently as she nodded and turned her horse, motioning me to follow. The black dog at her feet gave a low woof and wagged his tail softly before turning after them.

When we reached the edge of the farm yard The Lady paused and looked down at me fondly. "Thank you," she said in a surprisingly gentle voice. "Thank you for protecting Ruth and my farm. I owe you a debt and I won't forget that. I will be there for you when you're most in need."

I didn't know what to say to that but before I could answer both she and her companions turned and faded into the woods. Just as they were nearly gone, I thought I saw another shadow join them. A man on foot, who reached up and took the Dark Lady's hand in his. In another second they had disappeared entirely.

Sighing, I turned to the bleak scene that lay before me. The spot around where Bally and Alastair's bodies lay was crawling with police, firemen and emergency workers, and the night was coloured with flashing lights, lighting up the surrounding forest like a nightclub.

"Oi, Boss, looks like we have another one," someone yelled as I stumbled and nearly fell to my knees. Just before I hit the ground, I was caught in a pair of strong, familiar arms and crushed close to a strong, familiar chest where I could feel his heart pounding away like a jackhammer. The pain in my arm was intense but at that moment I hardly cared.

"Jilly," was all he said, in a voice full of love and fear, and I tilted my head back to look into his familiar eyes, realizing all at once how much I loved him. I'd always loved him, and that whatever I'd felt for Frederick was just a pale imitation of the real thing.

"Gil," I whispered and then his lips were on mine, soft like velvet, warm like spring rain, and powerful like all the forces of nature breaking over our heads. Time stood still and when he finally pulled back, he was looking at me with such love and pain in his eyes that I could hardly stand it.

"Gil," I said again, "I have to tell you something."

"Wait." He pushed me away gently, still supporting me but putting a little distance between us. He rubbed a hand across his eyes. "Jilly, I've been meaning to tell you something for a long time. Since we were kids. I should have never kept it from you."

"It's okay," I interrupted quickly. "I know. I … I love you, too."

He went stone still and then heaved a deep breath, bowing his head a little as if a great weight had settled itself over his shoulders.

"Jilly. Let me say this. I'm so sorry. I didn't know how to explain it properly without losing you. I want you to know that it doesn't change the way I feel about you. I've loved you since the first time we met. I want you to believe that."

"Of course, I do," I interrupted, "I've felt the same …"

I stopped as he held up his hand. Over his shoulder, I saw two EMT's wheeling a stretcher toward me over the bumpy ground.

"Jilly, when I was too young to understand what it meant, your mother came to me and tried to strike a bargain."

I froze, staring up at him in disbelief, my heart sinking.

"She said that she was worried about you and wanted me to be your friend, to pay special attention to you and make sure you never felt lonely. Of course, we were already friends so I didn't see anything special about that. Then she said that as long as we were friends that she'd let my father keep his job and allow me to ride and show the horses."

"No," I said in shock. "She couldn't have."

"She did. I didn't like your mother, she was scary even back then, but at the time I didn't see that I was doing something wrong."

"She … she paid you to be friends with me?"

"That was her plan," Gilbert said uncomfortably. "I was seven years old, Jilly, all I knew is that the scary lady wanted me to be friends with you or she'd fire my dad. I was *already* friends with you. I thought you were the most wonderful, interesting person I'd ever met. It was easy to agree to that."

"How long did it go on?"

"That's what I'm trying to tell you, Jilly, it never ended. She came to me every couple of years to renew the bargain. As I grew older, I became more and more aware of how wrong it was, and I told her that. She changed the stakes: my dad and I would be sent away, or she'd send you away to boarding school. The worst part was when she fired Nanny. I told her then that I wouldn't do it anymore, but she told me she'd send you away to school in Switzerland and I'd never see you again. I could see how miserable you were and being sent away from your home and the horses would have killed you. It was selfish, I know, but I also wanted you there with me. You were my best friend and I couldn't have imagined life without you."

"So that's why she let us have so much freedom together? That's why we could have sleepovers and she let you roam the house?"

"That's right. She made it very clear that I was never to assume that I fit in there, that I was only an employee."

"Oh, Gil," I said, torn between anger at my mother, horror at his betrayal, and sympathy for the young boy he'd been. After the terrible things that had happened that evening, it was too much to think about. In one night, I had lost the two things I loved most in the world. And yet…

"This doesn't change how we feel about each other, Jilly," he said earnestly. "Don't let her poison that for you. I always loved you best."

I thought about that as the light from the police cars began to fade and there was a strange roaring noise in my ears. There was an odd shattering feeling inside my chest and I realized, just before I hit the ground, that it was the sound of my heart breaking.

Chapter 19

When I next opened my eyes, I was in the hospital, tucked safely under a set of pale blue sheets. My arm was in a full-length cast and I felt like I'd slept for days. I was alone and that was a relief because I felt like I had so many things swirling around in my head that I would need a million years alone to process them.

Bally was a ghost. And Gil was... But that was as far as I got before the door was flung open and Mother herself pushed inside with a dramatic fling of her arm. I was slightly pleased to see that she looked awful. Her face hadn't been made up at all and her hair was pulled back into a rough ponytail rather than the jeweled clips she usually favoured.

"Jillian," she cried, in a ringing voice that made me wince, "What a dreadful place to spend your birthday in. We must get you out of here at once. I'm so relieved that you're alive. I couldn't believe it when I heard what had happened. Your father is on the next plane home from Rome; he was frantic when I told him the news. Are you ... are you all right, darling?"

There was a nervous catch in her voice, and I realized right then that she knew everything; not just Alastair and the wills, but about the return of my gift as well. And about Gil. And that there was a part of her that was afraid of what I might do.

"Hello, Mother," I said, stiffening against her sudden, awkward embrace. She pulled back; her eyes hooded as she looked at me warily.

"It was for your own good, Jillian," she said before I could say a word. "All of it. If you had a daughter of your own then you'd understand. Everything I did was to protect you. You ran wild, you didn't have any friends, the other children taunted you ... you were headed for a life of misery. It was a simple procedure that wasn't supposed to hurt. That gift was useless, how was I to know you wouldn't develop another one?"

"You're supposed to see the future, Mother; apparently you're famous for that talent. You're supposed to know how everything will turn out and you're supposed to not tamper with gifts that weren't yours to mess with."

My anger simmered and I glared at her until she was forced to look away. "You knew I saw ghosts right from the beginning. That it was real and I wasn't crazy. You pretended there was something wrong with me and then you fired Nanny, who was more like a mother to me than you ever were. Did you know that she *died* right after you fired her?"

She drew herself up to full height and I could see she was about to launch into one of her outraged protests.

"Your precious nanny was a crazy old bird who encouraged you to be a little hooligan; my only regret was that I didn't dismiss her earlier. Oh, Jillian, when you have children of your own, you'll understand. I've always looked out for you and your best interests. And my precognition doesn't work like that. I wish I could see everything but I can't. I would have never let you go to Dark Lady Farm if I'd known it would turn out like this. When I saw what was happening to you tonight, I nearly lost my mind not being able to help you."

"It was you who called the police, wasn't it?" I said, leaning back against the pillows. "The sirens started right after Alastair and ... and Bally were killed. There was nobody else who would have been able to do it."

"Of course, I did. It was the only way I knew how to help. I never trusted that Alastair. That whole family has a wicked streak a mile wide. I am truly sorry about that horse, Jillian. I know special he was to you. As soon as you're better we'll go shopping for a suitable replace—" She took a hasty step back when she saw the look in my eyes.

"Get out," I said quietly, my voice steady. "I'll see you when I get home. And if you so much as think of firing Christoph, or Gil, or buying me another horse then I will tell the entire family what you and Dr. Crane did to your own child. I'll take out an ad in the paper if I have to. I will go on national television. I know lots of our richer, more important, relatives wouldn't approve of your little "intervention."

She opened her mouth as if to say something further, but I pointed to the door and, grudgingly, she turned and flounced into the hall.

I lay back in bed and stared at the ceiling, exhausted by just a five-minute conversation with the woman.

A few minutes later the door opened again and it was Xan who poked his head in this time.

"Can we come in?" he asked with a wan smile. He turned to usher Estelle and Belinda in ahead of him without waiting for an answer and then held the door open so two more people could totter into the room.

"Aunt Ruth!" I cried, sitting up in amazement as she walked slowly to my bedside, leaning heavily on Jacob's trembling arm. "You're alive!"

Everyone was smiling down at me as Ruth walked slowly to my bedside and then leaned down and gave me a gentle kiss on the forehead. "Thank you, dear," she said softly in a nicer voice than she'd ever used with me, "for everything."

"Yes, Jilly, you're a hero," Estelle said, crutching over to stand beside Xan. "You saved Ruth and the estate; you saved all of us."

"I guess you're all right," Jacob added gruffly, almost smiling at me, "and I *am* sorry for hitting you."

"But how are you okay, Ruth? How did you wake up?"

"It was that Aimee," Belinda said indignantly. "She was drugging our Ruth that whole time with one of her concoctions. We found a veritable laboratory of potions when we searched her room. Dr. Crane said he'd never seen anything like it; he's taken them all back to his lab to determine what they were used for but we all know that it wasn't for anything good."

Aimee, I thought, remembering the gunshots and the way her body had hit the ground. I felt a throb of sadness.

"She's run away," Estelle went on. "Her clothes and purse were gone and she left a note apologizing for everything."

"But she couldn't have… she was shot," I said. "Alastair shot her right in front of me. And then the next moment she had disappeared."

They all exchanged a look of concern.

"There wasn't any evidence of that, Jilly," Xan said slowly. "There wasn't any sign of her at all. Are you sure you saw Alastair shoot her?"

"Yes," I said quickly, and then paused, remembering the way her body had just sort of faded away. What other powers had Aimee had at her disposal? For all I knew she could live forever. "And Alastair, is he really dead?"

Xan's eyes filled with sudden tears. "Yes, the police made a brief attempt to revive him when they arrived but it wasn't any use. The ambulance attendants said he probably died instantly when the horse fell on him."

The horse. I looked away not ready to talk about Bally.

"Xan, I'm so sorry that it was Alastair... does Sally know yet?"

Xan smiled bleakly and sighed. "She's not taking it very well, I'm afraid. He was always a strange person but I never thought he'd do something like this."

And he killed your parents, I thought, wondering if Xan knew that yet. I also wondered how much Sally had been involved in everything.

"We have an announcement," Xan went on, his smile a bit happier. "I'm going to stay on at Dark Lady Farm and help Estelle and Great Aunt Ruth with the horses. They have some real top-class contenders there and I'll need something to ride while Rigel goes into remedial training."

"Oh, Xan, that's wonderful," I said, noting the way Estelle's hand rested so naturally on his shoulder. I had a feeling that everything would work out just fine for those two.

"Estelle will need extra help with the estate while Jacob and I are on our world cruise. We're celebrating our honeymoon in style," Aunt Ruth said, her face wreathed in smiles. I hardly recognized her now that she was happy for the first time since I'd known her.

That could have been me wasting nearly my whole life, I thought bleakly, *without my gift, without love; I might have become just like she was.*

"You are, of course, welcome to stay on too, Jillian," she said, looking at me with the keen, eagle-eyed look I remembered so well. "You have made a great sacrifice on my behalf; the loss of your horse isn't something that can be measured in dollars."

She patted me on the arm sympathetically as my eyes filled with tears.

"That is a debt I can probably never repay. But, since I don't like owing people favours, I can offer you a free place to live while you get on your feet. You could get out from under the thumb of your controlling mother, do your dancy-prancy dressage, and have access to some of the finest horses in the world. What do you say to that?"

I stared at her. Here was a chance to escape my suffocating home life and the woman who had forcibly suppressed my gifts. But Nanny had told me that I wasn't finished with Greystone yet. There was something more I had to do there before I left for good.

I thought of the rolling fields and the stable full of good horses back home; horses that trusted me and were patiently waiting for me to return. And Christoph who was the best trainer anyone could hope for and then, of course, there was Gil. I wasn't entirely ready to forgive him. Not yet, but I knew that one day I would be. And Nanny and Bally would be with me, in one form or another. I wasn't ready to give it all up yet.

"Thank you, Aunt Ruth, for everything, but I think it's time I went home, at least for the short term."

"I thought you might say that. Well, I've left a small token of my appreciation back at the house. I hope it will be the start of your new collection."

Oh, no, I thought, *it had better not be one of those awful Dark Lady sculptures. I don't think I can handle that.*

"Any time you need anything at all, Jillian, even if it's just a break from that mother of yours, you just call."

Chapter 20

*G*il, Morris, and I rode back to Greystone mostly in silence. I wasn't ignoring Gil on purpose but I felt lost in my thoughts and that exposed secret now lay between us like a wet blanket that neither of us wanted to touch. I still hadn't told him about the ghosts, but I knew I would once the time was right.

We drove straight through without stopping, there would be no fun roadside diners to eat greasy food at this time. Morris kept up a resounded purr almost the whole way home, his comforting bulk sprawled across my lap. He'd become quite the pampered house cat during our vacation. Mother was going to be horrified that I was upgrading him from the barn to my bedroom, but I was pretty sure that was about to be the least of her worries once I got home. There were a lot of things that would be changing.

We'd left the estate early that morning and now, as we neared home, dusk was falling and all the streets of Maplegrove were lit up against the darkness.

We passed the bookstore, a golden glow falling out the front door onto the street, and then we came upon MapleBrew.

Although it was nearly dinnertime, I inhaled deeply at the fresh smell of roasting beans.

"Stop the truck," I said, surprising Gil so that he hit the brakes without even questioning it.

"Wait here," I ordered, opening my door with my good hand and stepping stiffly out into the darkened street. I didn't care this time that we were blocking most of the road with our horse trailer. People would just have to wait.

I marched up to the coffee shop and paused as I laid my hand on the door, taking a deep breath to find my courage.

Open the door, I told myself, *this is your new life. You just have to be brave.*

"Hello," the girl behind the counter called as I slipped inside, "chilly night, isn't it?"

"Um, yes," I said, sending a quick look around the coffee shop. Only a few of the people who looked up looked familiar. And I didn't see any anger or pity on their faces. Just people quietly enjoying some dessert and good conversation. How much of my anxiety about the townsfolk despising me had been in my head?

"What will you have?" the girl asked in a friendly voice. She looked vaguely familiar but I didn't recognize her. *Hmm, Katie*, I thought, reading her nametag, *she must be a little sister of one of my old classmates or something.*

"Um, what do you recommend?" I asked, tapping my fingers nervously on my cast. I'd waited for this moment since the day after Frederick dumped me, and now I had no idea of what to order.

"All our coffee beans are roasted here and are delicious. Do you like bold flavours or more mellow?" she asked.

"Definitely bold," I said, deciding that that fit in with the new me. "Two coffees and some cinnamon buns, please. To go."

"Coming right at you."

I paid her and balanced the little travel carton containing our coffees and dessert in my good hand while the girl ran around to get the door for me.

"Thanks," I said gratefully, and then caught sight of the handwritten sign in the window. "Hey, are you hiring?"

"Yeah," the girl said, "do you know of anyone? One of our girls just quit and we need someone like yesterday."

"Um, maybe I do," I said thoughtfully, wondering if they'd be crazy enough to hire someone with a cast on one arm.

"Well, tell them to drop off a resume. We'll consider anyone."

I took my precious carton out to the truck where Gil was waiting, luckily without a lineup of cars behind him. He got out and opened the door, keeping Morris from leaping out into the street while I got in.

"This doesn't mean you're forgiven," I said, setting the carton down and handing him his coffee.

He grinned at me and I couldn't help but smile back. We would get back to our old friendship again, I was sure of it. And after that, who knew what would happen? We just needed time.

The imposing stone pillars of Greystone Manor came into sight and we drove slowly up the driveway to the stables. It was time for evening feed and the comfortable sound of horses rattling their buckets and munching hay filled the air.

I shifted Morris off my lap and slowly eased myself out of the truck, my stiffening muscles protesting with every step.

"Hello, everyone," I said, walking slowly down the barn aisle to make sure that the stalls were ready. I was answered by a chorus of welcoming neighs. I looked fondly at the horses as I passed, wondering who would ride them now that I was out of commission. I didn't know if I ever wanted to ride again now that Bally was, well... not living.

I stopped in Bally's open doorway and surveyed his thick

bedding and well-filled hay net with approval, glad that Christoph had agreed to my strange request. The stall beside Bally's was ready too and, satisfied, I limped back toward the truck.

Gil already had the trailer open and was leading the small, bay colt down the ramp, the little horse looking around in astonishment at his new luxurious surroundings.

"Welcome home, Damascus," I said, stroking his fuzzy neck. I was infinitely glad that Great Aunt Ruth had been referring to me starting a collection of live horses rather than her creepy Dark Lady sculptures.

He looked around wide-eyed and then let out a piercing neigh that was immediately answered back by half the horses in the barn. I walked with them and watched while Gil escorted the little colt into his new stall.

I felt a soft nudge against my shoulder and I turned to my other horse with a smile. "You'll have to take care of him, Bally," I whispered low enough so Gil wouldn't hear. "Make sure he minds his manners."

Bally went into his open stall door and looked around at his familiar home with satisfaction and then gave himself a shake from head to tail like an oversized dog. He came back out of his stall and headed down the aisle, looking over his shoulder at me as if to ask, *well, aren't you coming?*

I followed him slowly out into the driveway and then up the hill to our favourite spot, the grassy rise from which we could look down and see the house, the stable and the fields beyond all stretched out in the sunset. I sat down on the grassy bank and Bally dropped his head to graze quietly a few feet away.

I sat there a long time, marvelling at the strange turn my life had taken this past week. Despite all the awful, scary things that had happened, for the first time in years, I felt alive. Like that hollow spot inside of me was slowly being filled with warmth. I had no idea how much of my old gift would find its way back to me. But I knew now that I was willing to fight for it; to fight for *me*.

The evening grew colder and it was time to go inside.

Side by side, Bally and I walked across the half-frozen ground toward the barn to where Gil and Damascus were waiting.

The End (for now)

Acknowledgments

Thanks to my mother for sparking my love of mysteries, puzzles and enigmas. Every birthday and Easter morning I'd wake up with a clue taped to my pillow (or sometimes my forehead) leading me on a hunt to find my presents. The adventure was always half the fun.

About the Author

Genevieve McKay is the author of over a dozen books, and most of them are about horses. She is an avid rider, reader, tea-drinker, and solver of mysteries. She lives on the west coast of Canada with her family, her horses, and an assortment of barnyard animals such as dogs, cats, sheep, chickens and two half-tame ravens.

Reading and Resources

If you are enjoying the Greystone Manor series, Defining Gravity series or any of my other books, I'd love if you'd take a moment to write a review on Amazon, Goodreads or any of the platforms where they are sold.

You might also enjoy checking out the new Three Sisters Farm series!

You can keep in touch by;

Visiting my website at www.genevievemckay.com

Follow my pics on Instagram: @mckaygenevieve

Or join my Facebook author page: www.facebook.com/authorgenevievemckay

I also have a mailing list where you can stay up to date on new releases, promotions and giveaways.

https://landing.mailerlite.com/webforms/landing/d2s9l0

Greystone Manor Mysteries

The Curse of the Golden Touch

The Sting of the Serpent's Blade

Book Three (Coming Soon)

The October Horses Series

The October Horses

Facing The Fire

Keeping Chilly (Coming soon)

Defining Gravity series

Defining Gravity

Flight

Freefall

Riding Above Air

Touching Ground

Three Sisters Farm Series

Everyday Horses

Book Two (Coming Soon)

Short Stories and Collections

The Horses of Winter

www.ingramcontent.com/pod-product-compliance
Lightning Source LLC
LaVergne TN
LVHW011151080426
835508LV00007B/346